Shooting Action Sports

Shooting Action Sports:
The Ultimate Guide to Extreme Filmmaking

Todd Grossman

AMSTERDAM • BOSTON • HEIDELBERG • LONDON
NEW YORK • OXFORD • PARIS • SAN DIEGO
SAN FRANCISCO • SINGAPORE • SYDNEY • TOKYO

Focal Press is an imprint of Elsevier

Acquisitions Editor: Elinor Actipis
Associate Editor: Cara Anderson
Publishing Services Manager: George Morrison
Project Manager: Kathryn Liston
Assistant Editor: Robin Weston
Marketing Managers: Marcel Koppes, Becky Pease
Cover Design: Aaron Atchison of Farm Design
Illustrations: Max Forward

Focal Press is an imprint of Elsevier
30 Corporate Drive, Suite 400, Burlington, MA 01803, USA
Linacre House, Jordan Hill, Oxford OX2 8DP, UK

∞ Recognizing the importance of preserving what has been written, Elsevier prints its books on acid-free
paper whenever possible.

Library of Congress Cataloging-in-Publication Data
Application submitted

British Library Cataloguing-in-Publication Data
A catalogue record for this book is available from the British Library.

ISBN: 978-0-240-80956-4

For information on all Focal Press publications
visit our website at www.books.elsevier.com

07 08 09 10 11 12   10 9 8 7 6 5 4 3 2 1

Printed in China.

To my family. With love, and appreciation.

Contents

Preface

What is the difference between a camera operator and a cameraman?

In 2006, I found myself working on a TV show for Intuitive Entertainment with cinematographer I-Li Chen. He was the first person I had ever encountered who could not only sum up the difference but also the importance of this difference. His explanation was as follows:

"Camera operators shoot what they're told, when they're told; they are more or less a tool with little or no creative input. Cameramen are a bit of a director as well. They are always watching and listening to everything that is happening. They are looking for moments, feeling the energy in a room, and identifying the story in what they are shooting. A cameraman will always capture the best moments."

I-Li hit the nail on the head with this statement. I've always found that people like to keep one eye closed while shooting film and video. Now granted, there are circumstances in which this is best to do; however, I find that most of the time, you are better off leaving your "non-eyepiece" eye open. The reason is exactly what I-Li said. With your other eye open, you will be able to seek out and find not just other moments that are brewing around you, but you'll also see what is happening just outside the edges of your frame.

In the summer of 2006, at what *TransWorld SKATEboarding* referred to as "The Best Skateboard Contest Ever" — The Vans Pro-Tec Pool Party in Orange, California — 200 of the best top pro and retired old-school ramp and pool riders showed up to compete in the enormous concrete Combi Bowl. What ensued was total utter chaos, and it was great. For any cameraman attending this event, thousands of insane tricks were pulled, hundreds of perfect moments happened, and dozens of multiskater collisions occurred. At an event like this, or even at a crowded local skate park, many things are happening at once. You'll find it very helpful to keep both eyes open and see not only what is happening around your frame, but also what is about to happen in it.

Predicting and anticipating is perhaps the greatest talent a cameraman can acquire. Whether you're brand new to shooting action sports or you've been doing it for years, if you remember nothing else from this book, remember this: be a cameraman, not a camera operator.

As noted above, and as you'll see throughout this book, there are countless examples of camera tricks and techniques used at major and minor events around the world. Just remember that even if you're only shooting something in your backyard or hometown, these techniques still apply. Video, film, and digital tools are just that: tools — it's your eye, your style, and your creativity that will make what you shoot compelling.

This book will take you through all aspects of production focusing on action sports. From planning and preparation to editing and post-production, you'll get a solid understanding of the changing technology, camera techniques, and basic to more-advanced shooting principles that can be applied to almost every scenario you might encounter.

Acknowledgment

If you're reading this then that means you've opened the book, and for that, I am grateful. The cover of a book is like a movie poster; you've got one chance to hook the viewers and entice them in to get a little more. Of course, movie posters can cost hundreds of thousands of dollars to make and require large design teams. In the case of this book, Aaron Atchison of Farm Design did an incredible job with the cover. Thanks Aaron.

If the cover of a book is like a movie poster, then the book itself must be the movie; and for the chance to make it, I must thank Cara Anderson, Elinor Actipis, and everyone at Focal Press and Elsevier whose support and enthusiasm made it all possible.

Every great movie and even skate video has an amazing team of people behind them. So for their contributions of time, energy, knowledge, and support, I thank those below and pray that if anyone was left out, you know how much I appreciate you.

Chris Mitchell

Ed Henderson

Erin Glenn

Rob Cohen

Julie Dotson-Shaffer

Craig Caryl

ASA Entertainment

Moz Mirbaba & Bill Keily at Windowseat Pictures

Tad Lumpkin

Michael Sugar

Justin Ward

Paul Temme

Max Forward

A History of Action Sports and Filmmaking

An Introduction

There are more than 75 million action-sports participants in the United States today, and well over 100 million fans.[1] That number has been growing steadily since the mid-'80s, with no signs of slowing. So how does this affect you and your desire to shoot action sports? Significantly.

Action sports were introduced to the mainstream world in the late 1980s under the all too well-known term "extreme sports." In 1995, one of the worldwide leaders in sports, ESPN, saw value in this growing niche and quickly founded the Extreme Games. The ensuing years demonstrated enormous growth in all disciplines — from the top-rated aggressive in-line skating of the 1990s, to the acceptance of snowboarding into the Olympics, to the now-prominent Freestyle Moto-X. ESPN and the world have continued to watch as more and more kids participating in conventional sports have steadily shifted to action sports.

Mainstream participation in this growing industry eventually led to an oversaturation of the term "extreme sports." ESPN soon amended

---

[1] Superstudy of Sports Participation conducted by American Sports Data, Inc., which monitors more than 100 sports and fitness activities.

the formerly titled Extreme Games to the now-massive X Games. Meanwhile, what began as a "go for broke" attitude among action-sports participants was maturing into a calculated approach to executing tricks and substantially lowering injury rates. The result was the evolutionary step of kids quickly progressing from being extreme-sports participants to action-sports athletes.

Flash to 1999. Tony Hawk stands atop an X Games vert ramp. Hundreds of cameras, professional and personal, look onward as the Best Trick finals timer counts down to the very end and Hawk fails to land his trick. Then, like a classic Hollywood story of a man fighting against all odds, with the contest over, Hawk continues to attempt his trick — again and again and again. The 900 (spinning two and a half times in the air) was a virtually unheard-of maneuver in skateboarding. If anyone was going to land it at such a prestigious event, it was going to be the godfather of the sport, Tony Hawk. Nearly every other athlete stopped skating out of respect and support for Tony. Then, after 18 failed attempts — with his fans, peers, and millions of people watching on television — Hawk dropped in once more, set himself up, and took off spinning blindly into the air. As he came around on the second rotation, this time Tony saw his landing, put his feet down, and rode away, executing the first ever 900 at the Summer X Games.

Hundreds of fans were rolling video that day. ESPN broadcast the clip to tens of millions of homes worldwide. When all was said and done, Tony Hawk's determination had managed to elevate skateboarding more than any other single event in action-sports history. Hawk went on to build the multimillion-dollar franchise that is his name today.

The broad appeal of this event may have been made mainstream through the cameras ESPN had rolling that day, but the significance of the event revolved around one simple thing: a guy on a plank of wood trying to land a trick that few thought possible. It doesn't matter if you're shooting with 14 cameras on cranes, cables, and dollies, or if you've got a basic digital-video (DV) camera from your local electronics store. It is the heart and emotion of any trick that makes it a great moment to capture.

Figure 1-1 *Dustin Miller at the LG Action Sports World Championships.*

Defining Action Sports

For the purpose of this book, I'll use the term "action sports" rather broadly. Many will claim that action sports are only the aforementioned "extreme sports," which include the following:

Skateboarding	Surfing
Snowboarding	Wakeboarding
Freestyle BMX	Freestyle Moto-X
Aggressive Inline Skating	Parkour

However, action sports can be far more than just the popular core sports. Although Webster's defines action sports as "any athletic endeavor considered more dangerous than others . . . ," and even Wikipedia attempts to define action sports, there are no officially defined limitations or boundaries as to what makes one activity an action sport and another not. For example, skiing has rarely been thought of as an action sport, but if you watch the Winter X Games, you'll now see countless young athletes hucking themselves off snowboard-sized kickers to do corkscrews and 900s, and even sliding the rails and boxes made popular in snowboard parks.

So what makes snowboarding a different action sport from skiing, which has kept its reputation as being a more mainstream sport? For starters, one of the ways many sports have been deemed "extreme" or "action" is based on the era in which they became popular. As an example, snowboarding is one of the quintessential Generation X and Y sports that has now been embraced by all generations.

Some, like *Webster's,* would claim that one way to define an activity as an action sport is by the level of danger involved. Interestingly, statistics have clearly shown that the believed danger in action versus conventional sports simply isn't true. On average, most action-sports athletes, such as skateboarders, are far less likely to receive any serious injuries than are football or basketball players. In 2005, skateboarder injuries averaged 23 per 1,000 participants, versus 38 per 1,000 participants of basketball.[2] Either despite or because of its reputation as "dangerous," the action-sports industry has settled into a stable coexistence with conventional sports. More often than not, events such as the Winter X Games skiing disciplines are being considered action sports.

Lastly, action sports can be identified by their progressive nature. There is often no clear-cut finish line; rarely can you judge winning or losing beyond pure subjectivity, and you'll often hear professional judges throw around words such as "style" and "creativity." These sports are always changing, always progressing. Even the best athletes in the world

---

[2] Statistics from the Consumer Product Safety Commission.

can't do every trick. Although big names such as Dave Mirra, Bucky Lasek, and the Yasutokos are considered top athletes in their respective sports, that doesn't stop a kid living in Anytown USA from inventing and naming a trick of his own. A huge part of the broad appeal of action sports is the chance to challenge the creativity of all participants, new or old, coupled with the opportunity to do so on an individual basis rather than as a team.

Illustration 1-1 Action sports vs. conventional sports.

Categorizing What You Shoot

For the purpose of simplicity, I've chosen the term "skaters" to use most often here and throughout the book when describing action-sports athletes. Keep in mind that all action-sports participants in every activity can be substituted on some similar level.

On a simple level, most skaters consider themselves street, park, or vert skaters. However, even subcategories exist within professional action-sports athletes: for example, video and magazine skaters, contest skaters, and big-trick skaters. The differences are as follows:

Video and magazine skaters are most often street skaters who are well respected for their technical grind, slide, and flip tricks. These pro skaters usually film parts for the upcoming videos over the course of weeks or sometimes even months. A trick here and a trick there — they are doing the most progressive and best of what's out there. Because these trick skaters are often doing such technical or difficult tricks, it can sometimes take them 10 or 20 tries to make their latest trick. This, of course, isn't true of all athletes — but more often than not, if you're shooting this style of skater, be prepared to stay involved with them for a number of tries. We'll dive into this more in the section on cameraman/athlete etiquette.

These "video skaters" are usually featured in annual or quarterly released skate videos such as *411 Video Magazine* or their latest upcoming pro-team video. They may have a few tricks in a music-driven montage section of the video, or they may have their own section consisting of dozens of tricks all cut to a single song. Either way, these skaters are not seen as often on television, and thus don't usually have the mainstream awareness that contest or vert skaters have.

This brings us to the next group of athletes — the contest skaters. These athletes pride themselves on consistency, and though they don't all like to admit it, they usually have some form of mainstream appeal. Standing atop a 17-foot-high roll-in with no one else on the ramp as half a dozen cameras shoot you for TV, and thousands of people in the crowd watch live, is no easy feat, and it's certainly not for everyone. Top contest athletes such as Brazilian skateboard X Games gold medalist Sandro Diaz or world champion in-line skater Eito Yasutoko have made a career out of sticking their tricks back-to-back ten out of ten times. These athletes are usually ramp (or transition) skaters, and wind up with some of the bigger endorsement deals, given the number of eyeballs that see them on TV versus the number of kids watching skate videos at home. The downside, however, is that it takes a good skate park to practice at, and not every city has one — whereas almost every town in America has a decent handrail and parking lot curb that people can session on.

Figure 1-2 Andy Mac sticks a frontside blunt (photo by Todd Seligman).

Last are the big-trick skaters. These are the athletes that first made a name for themselves by doing huge — or what some might consider crazy — stunts. These are the guys or girls who virtually redefine the word "extreme" with what they do. Be it street or ramp skaters, park or backcountry snowboarders, or even downhill mountain bikers, in every action sport, there are a handful of people pushing themselves to — and often beyond — the edge of calculated risks. In 1995, Freestyle BMX legend Mat Hoffman built a 25-foot-high quarter-pipe in his backyard and was towed into the ramp across a plywood runway by a street motorcycle. His 42-foot air is in the *Guinness World Records*. In

1998, in-line vert skater turned pro snowboarder Matt Lindenmuth landed the first ever — in any sport — double backflip on a vert ramp. Finally, the pioneer of the X Games Big Air event, Mr. Danny Way himself, had VPI Industries reconstruct his mega-ramp in Beijing, where a lifetime of impressive athleticism culminated in Way's jumping the Great Wall of China — and in many respects, he's just getting started.

Figure 1-3 Danny Way's Great Wall of China jump (courtesy Todd Seligman).

These athletes are professionals in their own right. In every sport, you will find athletes who will more or less fit into one of these categories. Occasionally, you will find the great ones who will cross over to two or even three of them.

To sum it up, the kids read the magazines and watch the skate videos, the world sees the contest skaters on TV, and almost everyone pays attention when a stunt is performed. Still, the question remains: What will you shoot?

Although there are athletes who encompass more than one of these categories, understanding how to shoot in different environments will help you create the shots you want. In later chapters, we will review techniques and methods for shooting the different styles. The categories can — and do — expand far beyond the three main ones here; many athletes live outside of these, especially amateur and recreational athletes. Keep in mind that if your subject isn't a professional, he or she may not even be affiliated with any one category. But if you are shooting pros, then the following section will be a great help in understanding the pro-athlete mind-set.

Cameraman/Athlete Etiquette

When most action sports formed, they did so by chance, as more and more individuals fell in love with the sport and took it up. Very few, if any, professionals will tell you they started in their sport for the purpose of becoming a pro or making money. As a result, many people consider action sports more of a lifestyle than an actual sport. Because of this, if you attend a major contest, you'll see most athletes cheering for their buddies who are competing against them. Why? Because most riders compete against themselves, constantly trying to aggrandize their own ability levels and push their own limits.

Many cameramen go to major events or popular skate spots to shoot professionals, not necessarily knowing them personally. The most common mistake videographers and filmers make at these events is thinking that what they are doing is more important to the athletes than it usually is. So if you ever find yourself filming at a contest, demo, or any similar type of venue, keep in mind the following: if the event wasn't set up, and if the pros weren't flown in specifically for the purpose of your shooting them, then you are most likely not their priority.

If it weren't for the television and mainstream media coverage, these events wouldn't have the sponsorship dollars they need in order to take place. However, that's where the chicken-and-egg similarities end. In action sports, the footage we often get is dependent on our abilities to

Figure 1-4 Cameramen shoot pros at a contest.

work with or around the riders and what they are doing. Very often a pro rider will land a trick — and if you miss it, it's simply too late. The option always exists to approach the athlete and ask if they'll do it again for you. Many times, athletes will be fine with this as long as you ask politely and you're cool about it. Occasionally, however, they may be tired or just ready to move on. Of course, if you know the rider, this is a nonissue. It's when you don't know the athlete that it's important to be respectful. Imagine if it were you just doing something you love — and everywhere you go, people keep shoving cameras in your face and telling you what to do.

Pacing yourself for the sake of the athlete is also helpful. You can balance out how often you get in their face with the camera. Start farther back, then slowly work your way in. Take a break, then go farther back again. For example, if you have a wide lens, use it for those close-up action and character shots, but then take it off every so often and find a cool long-lens distant shot (more on this in Chapter 6, Shooting Techniques). This method will help a good deal in keeping the relationship between you and the athlete positive and respectful.

The second scenario may include your working with an athlete you know or have gotten to know at an event. If you set out to film a trick with someone specific, they will have certain expectations from you. There is a unique bond between cameraman and athlete that happens in action sports. In many respects, the entire dynamic shifts the moment they commit to getting a trick or many tricks for your camera. Like the video skater described above, athletes will try over and over again, working with you to get the trick on camera — whether it's for a video, a documentary, or even just the personal satisfaction they'll get from sticking it.

Skaters may look to you for encouragement to help keep them pumped up about landing a trick. This is where the bond forms. It becomes your job even as a cameraman to see that trick through as the skater tries over and over again. Although it's rarely said, it's disrespectful to walk away and stop shooting before a trick is landed if you've been invited to shoot it by the athlete. Keep in mind that of course this is not always the case, and most that athletes will understand if they've been at it for a while and you need to go. The key is to feel the energy, and if you want to stop, just be polite and ask.

I learned this lesson in reverse early on in my career when I was shooting a team video for Salomon in Europe. We were at a skate park in Germany, and I had been shooting video of various tricks and locations with the team all day. It was getting late in the evening, and I was tired. One of the athletes, Jake Elliot, was also a friend. Jake was trying a trick on the street course and working with me to get it on video. It was just the two of us. Like myself, Jake was getting tired. Eventually, I stopped getting excited, and it was more than clear to Jake that I was mentally done, trying to stay in it just for him. Finally, he approached me and said that he could tell I wasn't into it, and my lack of energy was bringing him down. He suggested I go crash and hand the camera over to a friend to help see the trick through. This was the first moment when I realized just how strong the relationship between athlete and cameraman can be.

Figure 1-5 *Athletes and cameramen.*

At any major event, the camera team is very often composed of a combination of professional sports cameramen and more-casual unobtrusive DV or high-definition-video (HDV) cameramen. In the late '90s, some athletes were very disrespectful to filmers. Early on in the sports, for every professional Tony Hawk type, there were at least two, if not more, unprofessional athletes. This latter category often said that the camera guys were there only because of them, and that therefore the cameramen should stay out of their way — out of sight, out of mind, if you will. But then the camera guys had the attitude of, "We shoot big events, and these are just some punk kids." The result was a lack of overall good coverage and a distant feeling from the athletes. People at home watching TV — or later, the event on DVD — may not have been able to identify what it was, but they could feel this separation. Eventually, most athletes and cameramen came to realize that these events weren't going away, and that if they work together, they'll get better shots on TV, which benefits everyone. Today, many athletes and cameramen are even great friends and go out together after the events. But the undeniable lesson learned here is, again, one of respect; it goes both ways and has to start somewhere. When skater and cameraman work together, the shots get more exciting, the material gets more compelling, and the odds of a successful shoot increase astronomically.

SKATEBOARDING IS NOT A CRIME

Figure 1-6 Classic early '90s bumper sticker.

The Bumper Sticker Syndrome

When I was 8, someone handed me a bumper sticker that read, "Skateboarding is NOT a Crime." I remember thinking to myself; "I'd get in trouble if I put this on my dad's car." Of course, it wasn't until I grew up that I realized the irony in this. By then, skateboarding was no longer viewed as a crime — well, at least not as much.

There are more public and private skate parks in the United States than in any other country in the world — and the number increases every day. Dreamland is building massive concrete skate parks funded by taxpayers across the Northwest, Tom Noble's SPC began with the legendary Ratz Skatepark in Maine and now builds killer parks in the Northeast, and so on. The industry has come a long way since the '80s, when skateboarding began its biggest resurgence in history. Watching the Sundance Film Festival award-winning documentary *Dogtown and Z-Boys* will show you the birth of skateboarding, along with some great

13

filmmaking. It wasn't until the 1980s, however, that the sport finally went through what many hope was its final major hurdle of mainstream acceptance.

Like most industries, in order to garner the attention of the public, it's often thought that any publicity is good publicity. It took a catchy slogan on a bumper sticker — "Skateboarding is NOT a Crime" — to help do this for skateboarding, along with the small-town slogan of almost equal power, "Support Your Local Skateboarder." These sayings helped make some progress against critics who are still being fought today, although on a much smaller level. Just because it's done in the streets, and not in a field or on a court, doesn't make it a crime.

Figure 1-7 *Early 1990s skate park.*

An interesting twist on this came in the mid- to late 1990s when the popular aggressive in-line clothing company Senate decided to release an entire line with laundry tags that read on the back, "Destroy all Girls." In the case of Senate, whether this was an attempt at making their sport appear more outlaw, a simple marketing ploy for publicity, or even just a creative outlet for their designers, it put Senate on the news across the country. The company quickly issued an apology, discontinued the tags, and went on to break every one of their previous sales records.

It's clearly apparent that even bad publicity can be good, but it will always take an event as positive and as significant as Tony Hawk's 900 to make any lasting impact. The public's opinion of the industry is shaped by how that industry is presented in the media. Although marketing schemes and bumper stickers have helped create public awareness, it's what you film and how you present it that will most often shape how people view that sport.

Modern Forms of Filmmaking

The argument goes like this: one filmmaker says, "3-D is going to save the movie theaters," then the other argues that "nothing will save them as downloading and home theaters get better, faster, and cheaper." Either side you take, there's no denying that a once-standardized industry is going through enormous changes for the first time in history.

Since the early 1900s, cameras and filmmaking have been relatively unchanged, with the exception of sound and color being added in. Now, almost 100 years later, we are witnessing the first technological advancement in filmmaking, and it's happening at blistering speeds. From Betamax video to DV cameras, HDV, and high definition (HD), there's no doubt that you now have choices out there in what you shoot. Chapter 2 will dive into these options more completely.

The face of filmmaking is becoming that of a faster, easier, cheaper medium that is resulting in more and more people picking up cameras to shoot their first — or 100th — short film or action-sports documentary. The result is more, better films and videos on the web and in stores.

Independent filmmaker Robert Rodriguez *(Desperado, Spy Kids)* is in many respects the best do-it-yourself filmmaker of our time. He has pioneered technologies in films such as *Sin City*, and has shown us that big-budget action films (for example, *Once Upon a Time in Mexico*) can be shot on high-def digital cameras near single-handedly. Rodriquez is notorious for writing, shooting, directing, producing, editing, and scoring his own films — basically a bigger-budget version of what many

Figure 1-8 *Robert Rodriguez on the set of* Planet Terror (Grindhouse) *(courtesy Dimension Films, photo by Rico Torre).*

action-sports filmmakers are doing today. You buy a camera, come up with a concept, shoot it, cut it, and — voilà — your own film that you can distribute on the web or on DVD.

On the flip side, many TV networks are keeping their structures of large film crews, and are just switching the format of shooting to adapt these faster, cheaper technologies such as DV, HDV, and HD. In both cases, the cost is coming down, and the quality is going up. This means that if your filmmaking is more than just a hobby, if you do any level of production with intent to distribute, then you are more and more likely to find success as studios and networks open their arms up to unestablished filmmakers such as once-unknown Robert Rodriguez.

The modern forms of filmmaking are still evolving, so if you want a leg up, it is key to stay current with the technologies. Just remember: anyone can read the manual from the newest camera and then press that red button and start operating, but that doesn't make them a cameraman.

The Tools of Action-Sports Filmmaking

Camera Gear: Choosing a Format

DV magazine, online forums, advice from friends . . . whom do you listen to when it comes time to buy a new camera? There's a lot of good advice out there, but the first question you need to answer clearly is, What do you intend to shoot, and is it recreational or professional?

Whether you're buying your first camera or just getting a new one, there is one significant difference in recent equipment offerings: some record to linear videotape, and some to internal hard-disk drives. Being that the latter technology is fairly new, many people still like the tangible comfort and simplicity of finishing a shoot and putting a physical tape in their pocket. Hard-disk-recording cameras are a growing phenomenon, and professionals agree they will someday replace linear-tape cameras, especially as disk storage capacity and reliability increase, and the costs of such technologies goes down. Hard-disk-capable cameras (see Figure 2-1) also offer instant access to scenes, just like a DVD would, and you can easily drag and drop clips to your computer from the camera. The downside? Disk cameras typically offer lower storage capacity, so you'll need to stop shooting and offload the content before you continue. If you are planning on shooting an action-sports event, or anything that will run a few hours or more, you'll likely need to shoot with a tape-fed camera. However, if you're shooting a short film or any other "controllable" event, a hard-disk camera should be sufficient for you.

Figure 2-1 Panasonic's AG-HVX200 with P2 media cards.

The most widely accepted and reliable tape-fed camera format is DV, or digital video. Sony, Panasonic, Canon, and JVC all offer a great array of variably priced reliable DV cameras. The DV format shoots at a native 720×480 lines of resolution (see Table 2-1). Cameras that shoot DV will still vary in quality, though, based on a variety of other factors — most notably the number of CCD (charge-coupled device) chips they have and the quality of the optics. Cheaper DV cameras are single-chip devices — that is to say, they have a single CCD chip that converts all color information to tape. Higher-end cameras are three-chip devices; they have three CCDs, with each one designated to record part of the RGB spectrum (one for green, one for red, one for blue). Many years ago, DV wasn't considered a passable medium for broadcast-television work, but with the proliferation of reality TV and other forms of lower-budgeted filmmaking, three-chip DV cameras have become more widely accepted for professional use. In fact, you'd be surprised how many live-action sporting events will broadcast mixed-camera formats. I spent approximately six years shooting bike, skate, and in-line events for ASA Entertainment. Most of those events were broadcast on Fox Sports or ESPN. Very often the shoots would consist of from four to six ENG (electronic news gathering) Betacam cameras and one or two DV cameras that would focus on getting in the action and more-personal shots with the athletes. Although there can be a noticeable difference in the looks of those two formats, oftentimes we'd use that difference to our advantage. For example, when we shot ASA events, we would use a DV camera (then a Sony DCR-VX2100 or similar) as the on-course followcam while the Betacam SP cameras stayed fairly stationary. This meant that every time the show producer would cut to the followcam, it was a unique and exciting angle that also had a unique look to match.

In the world of action-sports videos, three-chip DV and HDV cameras are the number one camera format used across the board. They offer a small, unobtrusive package for getting in close and personal with your subject, as well as getting the camera quickly and easily into and out of high-risk shots. Let's say you want to shoot someone grinding down a handrail on the street or along the coping of a ramp. The compact size of a DV or HDV camera will allow you to stand relatively close, and you'll find it much easier to step back to safety if your subject messes up and you suddenly find a bike, board, or person flying toward you. I can't even begin to count the number of times I've had a camera within inches of a skateboard or the pegs of a bike as someone lost control of a trick and I had to pull my camera out extremely quickly. Most three-chip DV and HDV cameras, such as the ones listed below, even have a sturdy handle located on the top for easy operation.

19

One of the primary techniques used in filming action sports is to throw on a wide-angle lens, open the LCD screen, and hold the camera close to the ground, using the handle on top. My disclaimer: just remember that getting in close to your subject while they're spinning, flipping, or grinding is always going to put you and/or your camera at risk. About eight years ago, I was shooting a skater in Puerto Rico for a video called *Hoax 7: Scared Straight*. I was following the skater at fairly high speed, down a sheet of wood that covered a set of stairs as part of his line through a park. Every time he would mess up and we would do it again, I felt a little more comfortable and would get a little bit closer. The problem arose on the fifth take. I got so close to him that just as I was jumping onto the wood, he was also landing on the wood — causing it to bow up at the ends. The result was that the 3-inch lip was now more like 8 inches, and my wheels caught the edge — which sent me flying forward, camera first. I managed to hold on to the camera and protect it, as I rolled out of it getting some scrapes on my elbows and back. The lesson here is twofold: first, having that handle on top saved my camera, enabling a strong enough grip to not lose it midflight; and second, no matter how many times you shoot something in what feels like a controlled environment, things change. So keep your eyes open.

Table 2-1

	DV	HDV	HD
Picture Size[a]	720 × 480	1440 × 1080	1920 × 1080
			1280 × 720
Average Data Rate	25 Mbps	35 Mbps	100 Mbps to
			440 Mbps
Sampling Rate	4:1:1	4:2:0	4:4:4
Pixel Resolution	345,600	1,555,200	2,073,600

Note: This table represents only some of the most commonly used formats.

[a]Resolution is based on the NTSC video standard used in the United States.

DV Cameras

The DV format was created by a group of ten or so companies, including many of the big dogs (Sony, Panasonic, JVC, Philips . . .). DV was originally designed as a fast, cheap, and simple replacement to less-reliable formats such as 8mm and Hi8. DV, however, records only onto a ¼-inch tape. This means that the slightest scratch, ding, or pull can leave your footage with a digital hit, or even go so far as to ruin it entirely. Although DV has become so standardized, and its tapes so high quality, that this damage is rare, it is nonetheless very important to always keep your tapes stored in a cool, dry place. If you happen to shoot something irreplaceable, you may want to back it up before you begin playing and watching the tape repeatedly; DV tape will begin to break down as the camera or video deck heads repeatedly push against the tape during playback.

Another important feature to understand in DV is compression. Originally called DVC (digital videocassette), DV takes the information the CCD chips gather, and then compresses that video using a discrete cosine transform (DCT) in order to decrease the size of the digital stream of data. The compressed stream of data going to the tapes is only 25Mbps (megabits per second), as opposed to 100Mbps and up for true high definition. This amounts to a serious difference between tape formats in data rates and compression. Although DV looks good, you'll see the difference when you compare it to HD (high definition).

The first widely accepted DV camera came in 1995 when Sony hit the market with a prosumer camera that set the standard for everything to come, the DCR-VX1000 (see Figure 2-2). This three-chip DV camera still sells today in various incarnations, from the redesigned VX2100 series to Sony's first true 24p HDV (high-definition-video) camera, the HVR-V1U, which released 11 years later with a striking resemblance to the VX1000 (see Figure 2-3). What made the VX1000 so popular was its versatile design and serious durability, all at a reasonable cost. Action-sports athletes and filmmakers around the world quickly embraced this camera, and it became a staple of almost all action-sports video.

Figure 2-2 Sony DCR-VX1000, released in 1995.

Figure 2-3 Sony HVR-V1U, released in 2006.

HDV Cameras

The Sony HVR-V1U (as seen in Figure 2-3) uses the ever growing in popularity HDV format. This format records to the same tapes as DV, but uses a codec based on MPEG-2 (Moving Picture Experts Group) video compression, which enables a much higher compression rate than does DV. The downside to squeezing so much more information on the same size tape, as you may have guessed, is that more problems arise with dropouts and artifacting. Many people agree, though, that it's worth the sacrifice, based on the increase in overall quality that HDV delivers.

The HDV format is more expensive compared to DV, but it is worth it. With high-definition forms of DVD such as Blu-ray and HD DVD — as well as HD content available via cable, satellite, and the web — the outlets to watch your HD recorded material are becoming more regular every day.

One key perk to shooting HDV is that the cameras remain almost the same size as DV, and you can swap tapes quickly and easily. (Please see Chapter 9, Post Production, for the different needs of editing equipment for HDV.)

It's also important to note that almost all HDV cameras allow you to switch back into regular DV mode if desired. Most cameras also have a down-conversion feature built in, allowing you to shoot HDV, but then output DV into your computer for editing. This is a nice feature if you plan on archiving footage for down the road, but for now need only a lower-res edit for the web. Remember, although you may not have an HD television or Blu-ray DVD burner now, you will in the near future. My advice is to honestly look at where you intend to screen your work, and decide if HDV is worth the added investment. Most good three-chip HDV cameras can be had for a few thousand dollars, and go up from there.

HD Cameras

Many people assume that HDV is HD, and they're right, partially. By definition, an HD (high-definition) camera is one that shoots at a higher resolution than an SD (standard-definition) camera, such as DV or Betacam SP. However, I've chosen to separate HDV and HD because of the significant differences you'll encounter with both formats. Originally, the National Television Standards Committee, also known as NTSC, standardized the United States at 525 lines of resolution with 29.97 frames per second (fps). HD is usually shot with 1,080 lines of resolution and an aspect ratio of 16 × 9 (or 1.78 : 1), compared with conventional television's 4 × 3 (or 1.33 : 1) (see Figures 2-4 and 2-5). The 4 × 3 ratio of most television shows today is slowly being replaced by the widescreen format of movies and HD. Most plasma and LCD TVs come widescreen, as do more and more laptops these days because widescreen more closely represents what you actually see, and thus is more appealing to the eye. Even your DV and HDV camera will give you the option to shoot widescreen by either letterboxing the image or stretching it out to utilize all the pixels (called anamorphic), and then allowing you to resqueeze in postproduction, thus retaining a higher-quality image. One of the upsides of shooting 16 × 9 is the cinematic look and feel it creates.

Figure 2-4 *4 × 3 aspect ratio.*

Figure 2-5 *16 × 9 aspect ratio.*

Although true HD is nearly four times the resolution of standard def (see Table 2-1), it's also typically more than four times as expensive, so most action-sports videos are rarely shot on full-resolution HD. Some of the more popular HD cameras — such as the Sony HDW-F750 and HDW-F900, as well as the Panasonic VariCam and AJ-HDX900 — deliver amazing image quality and camera versatility. At the time of this writing, however, they still retailed for between $26,000 and $90,000, depending on the model. These cameras do feature interchangeable lenses and larger tape formats with options for better (or even no) compression compared with HDV cameras.

The key to the decision on the part of most action-sports filmmakers to shoot HD is usually budget. If you're not expecting to project your finished product on a movie theater screen, then even the dramatic increase in quality may not be necessary for your project. Again, Robert Rodriguez shot *Once Upon a Time in Mexico* on the Sony HDW-F900, and that was a big-budget Hollywood film.

60i or 24p

When NTSC became the official standard in the United States in 1953, television had committed to the 29.97 interlaced format. This is the standard still used today in almost all of North America. Although the rest of the world uses PAL or SECAM, U.S. TV and video cameras have stuck with NTSC. The format builds each frame of video in two parts as it interlaces odd and even scan lines from each of two consecutive frames of pictures. This is why, when you pause interlaced video, you often get a stuttering effect. In contrast, 29.97, also referred to as 60i (the total number of interlaced frames in one second, rounded up), gives you a very sharp, in-focus, "video look." This look is usually associated with news, home videos, and anything of that nature. Film, on the other hand, typically shoots at 24 frames per second without interlacing. This accounts for part of the smooth, more surreal look of film. So, like the progressive nature of action sports themselves, video cameras have now begun shipping with a 24fps mode that does not interlace the frames. This mode, often called 24p, scans and displays each frame of video in its entirety before progressing on to the next frame. The result is a much more filmlike image, but shot on video. A few of the first and most popular prosumer video cameras — such as the Panasonic AG-DVX100 and AG-HVX200, and the Sony HVR-V1U — allow you to switch between 60i and 24p modes. These cameras typically offer a 30p mode as well, which is ideal for action. Because 24fps can cause a little blurring in the action if your subject is moving too quickly, action-sports filmmakers often shoot 30p as a means to compensate while still maintaining that progressive-frame-mode look.

The creative choice between 24p and 60i can be a very subjective one. Whereas most high-end HD filmmakers will shoot 24p for the purpose of getting that film look, a lot of documentary and action-sports cameramen prefer 60i for the exact reason that others dislike it: the sharpness, clarity, and deep-focus ability are great for capturing the action.

In 2004, I made a documentary called *Harnessing Speed*. The subject was *Stealth*, a summer action sci-fi film by Rob Cohen (director of such movies as *Dragon: The Bruce Lee Story* and *The Fast and the Furious*).

We had looked at numerous camera setups for the shoot, but in the end decided to shoot 60i for all of the behind-the-scenes-style footage, and 24p for all of the interviews and wrap-ups. The reason was that the 60i would help give the footage that feeling of reality, like the news, and thus create a sense of urgency and risk in what we were shooting. Meanwhile, the 24p interviews would look softer and smoother, a way to add a little polish to the piece without affecting the 60i footage.

Brooks Ferrell, an action-sports DP (director of photography) and cameraman, has shot many of the Vans skate events for Windowseat Pictures. These events are not just about the amazing skateboarding and snowboarding tricks that are pulled off, but also the lifestyle and characters that are shown. Brooks likes to capture all of the lifestyle in 24p mode, and all of the action in 30p. In the summer of 2006, we shot the Downtown Showdown for Vans on the back lot of Paramount Pictures. This shoot consisted of six Panasonic AG-DVX100B cameras, all in 30p or 24p mode. Because the back lot of the studio resembles New York City's Lower Manhattan, the surreal film look was ideal for the cool laid-back lifestyle skate event it turned out to be.

Almost all cameras should eventually offer a 24p or 30p mode, so if you're looking for a new one with which to shoot action-sports events, documentaries, or short films, it would be a wise investment to get a camera that offers this feature.

Film vs. Video

No camera breakdown is complete without examining the option to shoot film. Whether it's Super8, 16mm, Super 16mm, 35mm, Super 35mm, or even the enormous IMAX-sized 70mm format, there is no denying the beauty of film — and the insane cost of it.

First, the limitations: it's expensive; you can't instantly review what you just shot; it's bulky, fairly time-consuming to reload; and of course, you usually need to transfer it all to a video format in order to screen it, edit it, or distribute it.

Now the upside: it looks absolutely amazing.

Figure 2-6 Vans Downtown Showdown, Paramount Studios back lot. Courtesy Windowseat Pictures.

Up until 1999, the University of Southern California's film school (the USC School of Cinematic Arts) had all students in their entry-level 190 course shoot Super8 film. Doing so not only gave you an appreciation of film, but it made you really think about what you were filming, how you were going to edit it, and whether or not you really needed that extra shot. I remember using a fold-up clothes-drying rack as a means to hang all of my shot and developed Super8 film clips. By the end of a day of splicing and taping film together, when you finally sling up your finished cut, you pay very close attention to what shots you missed, angles you wish you had got, and things you'll correct next time. Although the 190 course, and many like it around the world, now uses DV, the trade-off is the quantity of material you can shoot for mere pennies. Most of the higher-end courses at numerous film schools (including USC) do, of course, still offer 16mm and 35mm filmmaking, the standard in many Hollywood feature films.

Full 16×9 HD resolution (1920×1080), is just shy of what's called 2K (2048×1080); however, full 35mm film resolution of a theatrical film or digital projector is closer to around 4K (3656 × 1976). This is a big difference in quality. The larger the format of the film (8 mm, 16 mm, 35 mm . . .) the higher the quality; thus, IMAX's ability to showcase 70 mm film on a 60-foot screen.

Film also retains the capacity to easily create a narrow depth of field (or shallow focus). This is most often seen in personal or romantic Hollywood film moments when the actors are crystal sharp, but the background is extremely soft and blurry. Achieving this shallow depth of field on video is far more difficult, but can be most easily achieved by using longer (telephoto) lenses (more on this in Chapter 5, Camera Angles, Lenses, and Framing).

A final great perk of film is its latitude. Latitude is the range of light and dark areas that get exposed in your film, and it is far greater in film than in most video standards. This means that bright areas are less likely to blow out into white, and dark areas are less likely to just look black on film. Although all video cameras differ in the amount of latitude they offer, particularly for capturing low-light situations, it is a safe bet to say that none are as versatile as film. So from the overall quality and latitude, to the shallow focus and film grain, there are many reasons why film looks so good to the human eye.

If you want to test the waters with film, the cheapest and easiest means of entry is with a Super8 camera (see Figure 2-7). Often bought and sold for under $100 online in stores such as eBay, these cameras offer easy-to-use cartridges that just pop in and out, and can be purchased with developing and transfer packages from places such as Pro8mm in Burbank, California. Although a high-end Super8 camera with a nice transfer can yield a good image, many provide a very grainy and scratchy old-film look that many action-sports cameramen try to emulate with video shoots. You will find various old-film or Super8 filters that can be added to video during post; however, nothing as of yet will give you that true look of original Super8.

Film is still used in many big-budget action-sports films. Snowboarding and Freestyle Moto-X films, for example, very consistently shoot 16mm or Super16 film for enormous sections of the latest videos. The reason is because snowboarders and Moto-X riders usually go huge on

29

Figure 2-7 *Bauer Super 8mm film camera.*

every hit, so film makes sense. Whether they land it or crash, the stunt is probably going to make the cut. It's also fair to say that any higher-profile video can afford to shoot film. Skateboarding, BMX, and aggressive in-line are far more technical in comparison, and thus far less consistent. If you're rolling film on a skateboarder trying a very technical trick on a ramp or on the street, it may take countless tries before they land it — by which point you've burned through seven rolls of film . . . and your wallet. If you'd like to see a great example of just how good film can look with action sports, check out one of my all-time favorite sections in the Tony Hawk Birdhouse video *The End*, directed by Jamie Mosberg. This features numerous film segments that all culminate in an epic vert-ramp scene at an old bullfighting arena in Mexico. The music, the skating, and the cinematography all seamlessly integrate into a phenomenal section.

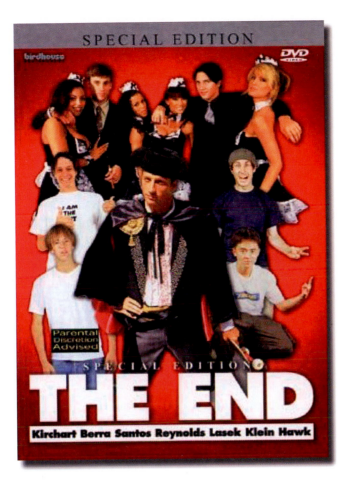

Figure 2-8 *Tony Hawk in the Birdhouse skate film* The End.

Sound Gear

If every video camera comes with a built-in microphone, then why should you worry about sound gear? This is a very fair question, and the truth lies once again in determining what you're shooting. For the average video hobbyist, the onboard mic will suffice. However, if you plan on distributing your video via DVD or the Internet, or if you just want it to look and sound better, then you may want to consider some aftermarket sound options.

A movie with bad sound is like a house with no roof — it's just not good. Anytime someone watching your video is struggling to understand what an athlete is saying, or the sound from the action seems chintzy or shallow, it'll be a distraction from enjoying the piece for what it should be. Great sound can be recorded in one of three common ways.

The first is often the easiest and most effective; it involves an additional, higher-quality, onboard microphone. Most cameras have a metal bracket or slot on top of them for mounting lights or microphones; this is where you'll attach most mics. Although you should always read reviews for the microphone you plan to buy, the most common choice for shooting video is a unidirectional mic (see Figure 2-9). This type of mic comes in numerous pickup patterns (the directions and intensity in which a microphone "hears" sounds). The two most common patterns for action sports and documentary shooting are found with the shotgun mic and the cardioid mic. My personal preference is the shotgun.

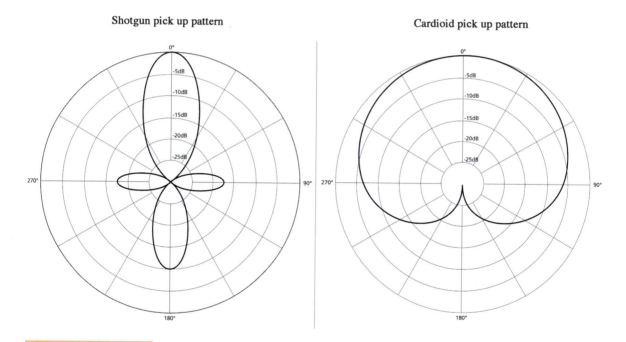

Figure 2-9 Common pickup patterns for microphones.

As you can see from Figure 2-9, the shotgun mic (named for its ability to cancel out audio from the sides and focus primarily on what's in front of it) and the cardioid mic (named for its heartshaped pickup pattern) are ideal for shots requiring you to focus on a single subject in front of you. If you need to get short sound bites or OTFs (on-the-fly interviews) from your subject while also shooting action in a dangerous environment, these light onboard mics are truly ideal for that "gun and go" documentary style. Prices can start as low as a couple hundred dollars for an entry-level microphone, and go all the way up to a few thousand and beyond. The Sennheiser MKH 416-P48 has been a staple of my arsenal for many years. It records crystal-clear sound and is able to focus in on one subject while shooting in loud environments. I've captured countless live events with only this mic mounted on my camera. At the Vans Cup in Northstar at Tahoe in 2006 and 2007, I recorded brief sound bites using this mic while snowboarders sat on the start box with music blasting, spectators screaming, and Mother Nature dumping. At a distance of 2 to 4 feet from the athletes, the sound quality was perfect and made most of the shots usable.

However, if you're doing followcam or anything that may be action-only oriented, you may opt to settle for the internal mic as a means to save weight and energy. Oftentimes the onboard microphone will give you all you need for action shooting; then you can use a mic for your interviews or more-personal moments. You will also have the opportunity to sweeten up the natural sound when you get into post (see Chapter 9).

The second way to mic is with a boom. Also known as a fishpole, this lightweight long arm can reach exceptionally far out to capture your subjects. Booms can then be either hardwired directly to your camera or to a wireless audio transmitter that can send the sound to a receiver attached to your camera. Booms usually get you better audio than an onboard shotgun mic because they generally get closer to your subject. The ideal scenario for booming is when the talent knows and expects you to be there, and you are recording multiple people interacting. The downside to the boom is its cumbersome size and obvious presence; it can be an enormous distraction to your subjects, and thus a hindrance to what you're shooting. I also wouldn't recommend it when recording action — the boom can get in the way and even become a dangerous obstacle for an athlete. The key to using a boom is a knowledgeable boom operator and a controlled environment. I typically boom only professional shoots in which the athletes are there to work with us for a specific goal.

Figure 2-10 *Boom mic versus lavaliere mic.*

The third and final technique is the lavaliere microphone (or lav or lapel mic). These are small dynamic microphones that clip or attach to the collar of your subject's shirt. They provide an excellent source of audio, but only for the person wearing them; don't expect to capture good sound from people standing next to your subject, though a little pickup will happen. These mics also take more time and energy to set up, so plan on making time to stop your subjects while you wire them and find a safe place to stash the transmitter — often the athlete's front pocket, where the mic is less likely to fall. Just remember to put in fresh batteries before you walk away!

One of the largest drawbacks to using a lav mic is that some athletes don't like the idea of being recorded when they don't see the camera around; there've been many stories of what Hollywood actors and professional athletes have said and done when they forgot they were mic'd . . . but we won't go there. As noted in the section on cameraman/athlete etiquette in Chapter 1, most talent simply doesn't like to be distracted or bothered when skating — and thus, lavs are out. If you are able to use lavs, just remember that they will also need to patch into your camera's first or second audio input; so if you need to mic more than one or two people, this may also be a hindrance. Most prosumer cameras do have at least two audio inputs, so patching one lav mic in and then using the second input for an onboard shotgun mic can work extremely well. There are also numerous third-party adapters (for example, from BeachTek) that can split single audio inputs into additional inputs. These adapters, however, may allow audio to "bleed" between channels — which can work for or against you, depending on the goal.

The U.S. Air Force and advertising agency GSD&M launched a campaign titled "Do Something Amazing" in 2006. I was fortunate enough to shoot and field-produce many of the broadcast and web spots with director Bill Kiely for Windowseat Pictures. Bill and I would spend countless hours at bases around the country, working with and filming real Air Force personnel who aren't used to cameras. Although we would always have a sound operator with a boom and lav close by, there were numerous instances in which we would use only the shotgun mics. The benefit was threefold: being untethered from a soundman, and thus able to move more quickly; being smaller in operation and able to get into smaller areas such as fighter-jet cockpits; or simply being able to remain unobtrusive and keep our talent acting naturally.

Figure 2-11 *Director Bill Kiely shoots a USAF walk-and-talk interview.*

So there are the three primary approaches to recording sound. You will have to consider if it's worth the expense for your projects, but I can't reiterate enough how much of a difference good sound will make. In my sophomore year of college, a USC professor wanted to demonstrate to us the importance of sound. He proceeded to show us the legendary Indiana Jones scene from *Raiders of the Lost Ark* in which Indy is running for his life from an enormous boulder careening through a cave after him. Presented in 35mm film on a large-format movie screen, the scene was every bit as intense and harrowing as I remembered it . . . that is to say, until our professor screened it again with only the original sound that had been recorded on set. Now you could hear Harrison Ford's heavy breathing, the hollow set echoing his footsteps as "Indy" ran, and that massive boulder sounding like the plastic prop it actually was. We watched that scene four times. Each time, we added a level of audio quality: first, the nat sound followed by the sound effects; then the music; and eventually, the full mix as it had been seen and heard in theaters. For me, the lesson would never be forgotten: sound can make up nearly 40 percent of a film. So the next time you're shooting your project and you consider slacking a little bit on the sound quality, just picture Indiana Jones running through a cave and being chased by a big old plastic rock.

Rigs, Mounts, and Specialized Gear

This section could cover a wide range of customizable gear. Instead, we're just going to focus on some of the more popular and practical toys: lipstick cameras, specialty mounts, dollies, Steadicams, and jib arms and cranes. Let's begin with the lipstick camera. Also referred to as a cigar cam, these small tubular-shaped cameras are now made by most of the big camcorder companies. For years, the most popular model was the Sony XC-999 ultracompact camera module.

Even today, with hundreds of other small cameras on the market, the Sony XC-999 has held its own with a high-quality RGB image and an extremely rugged and durable design. With 470 lines of resolution and

Figure 2-12 *Sony XC-999 camera module.*

768 × 494 pixels, as well as fully interchangeable lenses including tele-photo and fish-eye options, the XC-999 can be placed almost anywhere on almost anything. For a stunt motorcycle documentary called *The Outsiderz,* some friends and I mounted XC-999s on the bikes for all sorts of insane stunts and crashes; this added extra production value to the shoot by giving the audience unique angles they rarely get to see.

Mounting options for these cameras can be on an athlete's helmet, to the side of the bike, or even underneath a skateboard. Limited only by your imagination, some of the most creative filmmaking I've ever seen has employed the use of lipstick cameras and clever mounts. Most require an external record source, so plan to tether them to your video camera or a basic portable recorder, often called a clamshell. With HDV- and HD-resolution lipsticks slowly becoming more realistic on shoots, the quality of your work will also increase. One consideration, however, is that if you don't absolutely need to get the camera in a small spot, many consumer DV and HDV camcorders are now so small that they rival old lipstick cams. Rather than buying a lipstick camera and a recording device that will require mounting and cabling for both, consider these small camcorders as a very real option. Many record to tape or even internal hard disk, making them simple, compact, and perfect additions to your camera arsenal.

The more angles and coverage you get during your shoot, the more options you're going to have in the edit bay; thus the expression "cover-age, coverage, coverage." Always remember: if you don't get it, you won't have it.

Figure 2-13 Sony HDR-CX7 hard-disk camcorder.

Other unique ways to capture your subject include specialty mounts. Manfrotto is just one of many companies that make various clamps and mounts for all types of cameras. One unique mount is a suction cup that will adhere to most smooth surfaces, such as the side of a car or the nose of a snowboard. Because a mount can break free, I would always recommend safe tying. A simple rope or clasp can run from the handle of your camera to a secure point on whatever you've mounted to, ideally somewhere higher than the mount. That way, if it does break free, the camera will hang there, as opposed to hitting the ground and dragging. Suction mounts can be great for getting that killer point of view outside a race car or even on the side of a motorcycle.

One of my favorite types of clamps is called a Magic Arm. This fully articulated arm extends up to 20 inches, and features two elbows that rotate a full 360 degrees. By loosening an easily twistable knob, you can precisely align your camera, then twist the knob to lock off all the joints. Just note that with the arm fully extended, any serious movement or bouncing will shift the camera. I typically lock off a second arm to the top if possible; this creates a more stable triangle lock.

If you don't have access to these types of mounts, remember that you can almost always build your own using basic parts from a hardware store. For a Nissan 350Z spec commercial I made with pro skater Danny Way, I wanted to get a distinctive angle on the front of the skateboard as he power-slid to a stop. To make sure our small 16mm film camera would remain locked off relative to the board, we attached the camera using small hollow aluminum tubes and plates. It worked perfectly without breaking the bank.

Figure 2-14 *16mm GSAP camera mounted to pro skateboarder Danny Way's board.*

Lastly, let's talk about specialized gear such as dollies, Steadicams, jib arms, and cranes. All of these devices can add a serious level of production value to your shoot. Unfortunately, they can also cost a great deal, take a lot of time to set up, and be just about as obtrusive as it gets. The first immediate benefit of these rigs comes from the idea that your camera is moving smoothly. Many lower-budgeted productions are plagued with a tripod or handheld syndrome. Too many tripod shots, and your project can start to feel too static; too much handheld, and you'll need to give out Dramamine with copies of your film. The balance can come from doing both handheld and tripod (or lock-off) shots. Camera movement often creates intrigue, and adds a layer of complexity to your piece. Inexpensive jib arms and dollies are a great way to get

39

in some basic movement. There are ways to imitate this gear as well, and we'll talk about them more in Chapters 5 and 6.

The X Games and similar events love to use cranes, jibs, and even cable cams (cameras running along high wires over the competition course). Most large events avoid Steadicams and dollies because they require the operator to be too close to the talent, and they're often too smooth to be a main camera; they take away from the intensity of the tricks being performed by the athletes. These are all considerations that you'll have to tackle prior to your shoot. Just remember that the equipment pieces you choose to employ are nothing more than tools; you should never use a cool piece of equipment just because you can.

Editing Software and Hardware

When it comes to postproduction, you will have many options to choose from. In the old days, films were cut linearly by actually splicing and taping pieces of the film together. One of the many problems, however, was that every splice would require you to cut out a frame of footage, so there was no going back once the cut was made. In 1989, Avid introduced their first ever nonlinear editing system. Nonlinear editing (NLE) is a system that can access your original material at random without first going past the content that came before it (consider an audio CD compared to the linear requirements of an audiocassette tape). Avid, in its many forms, went on to become the staple of motion picture editing. It has remained the Mercedes of edit systems, and maintains a hefty price tag (well over $50,000 for its high-end complete turnkey system). Originally based solely on the Macintosh computer platform, the Avid is still used today by many Hollywood studios for editing, although its top competitor, Apple's Final Cut Pro HD (FCP), has been wowing professionals more and more with each new release.

A common misconception about FCP HD and FCP Express is that they can rival Avid for their low $1,200 and $299 price tag, respectively. This is only partly true. Final Cut Pro is software based, meaning that it runs on your computer from installed software and requires no additional tools or hardware (please read on, though, for FCP setups that do require some hardware). Hardware-based edit systems are typically far more powerful and may even offer more or expanded features. Avid now makes a software-only version of their system that is closer in price to FCP.

Figure 2-15 *Final Cut Pro HD nonlinear editing. Courtesy Apple.*

Apple computers have long been considered ideal for creative work such as editing, particularly for their user-friendly interface, intuitive design, and exceptionally crash- and freeze-resistant operating system. However, unlike Avid, which is available on both Mac and PC platforms, Final Cut Pro HD is solely for Macs. Today, there are more than 100 options when it comes to NLE systems.

Choosing the right one for you depends largely on your assets and intentions. If you have a PC, then one of the most popular systems, Final Cut Pro, is out. If you are on a tight budget, then Avid is likely not an option. You'll also want to consider what you're going to be editing. Many basic editing programs that come with computers, such as Apple's iMovie, are more than sufficient for basic edits and effects as long as you're capturing and working in DV or HDV. Also, companies such as Adobe, Pinnacle, and others offer inexpensive alternatives to the higher-end programs for your PC and Mac computer. I'd recommend searching what's new out there when it comes time to buy, and reading reviews on web sites such as CNET.com and PCMAG.com, where you'll find user and professional reviews of the latest software systems.

Next, you will want to consider what camera you are shooting on and what format you want to edit in. The most popular format for editing is DV, followed by HDV, which is growing in popularity. DV and HDV mean that you'll be able to connect your camera directly via FireWire 400 and 800 (also known as IEEE 1394), or USB 2.0 to your computer to capture (or digitize) the footage. DV as a codec, or type of compression, blew older formats out of the water when it was released, and has managed to hang on as the most used and sold camera and compression format to date. The downside to DV is twofold. One, its format is standard definition, not high definition. And two, DV will begin to break down in quality as it gets compressed and recompressed repeatedly. Imagine squeezing a bunch of your favorite clothes into a small suitcase. Now pass the suitcase on to someone who will put your suitcase inside of theirs, which just happens to be even smaller. If this goes on for a while, eventually, when you get it all back, your clothing is going to be far too squished and wrinkled to wear. Unfortunately, when it comes to DV, there's no way to iron it back to its original quality.

There is an upside to DV: it is extremely manageable in size, very inexpensive, and now used by the majority of all consumer and pro-sumer devices. To avoid the suitcase scenario, you can use a higher-end NLE system to capture the footage uncompressed. This means that, although the footage was originally compressed by the camera to fit onto the DV tape, you can uncompress it for editing, as opposed to recom-pressing it again and again. This technique, however, is where we get into more-complicated editing options (hardware and software based).

These days, many computers are fast enough and have enough storage to handle DV internally. But if you want to edit in uncompressed — or,

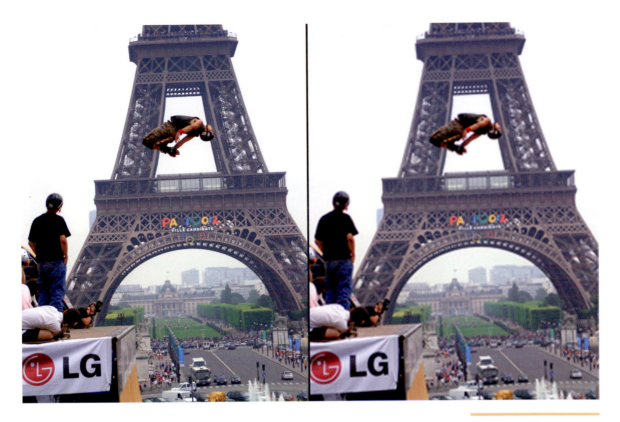

Figure 2-16

Uncompressed versus compressed video.

for that matter, in high def or any number of higher-quality standard-definition formats — you'll need the assistance of hardware. In order to handle the larger bitrates and data-file sizes of these formats, the higher-end Avid and Final Cut Pro HD systems will require additional external high-speed hard drives, SD or HD capture cards with optional breakout boxes, and sometimes even additional processor hardware boxes. These devices allow the real-time playback, editing, and layering of these data-intensive formats, typically too much for your computer to handle on its own. A faster hard-drive array may include two or more 10,000rpm drives striped together to help chomp on the data. These devices will sit in an enclosure that, depending on the format (Ultra-640 SCSI being one of the fastest), will then connect via cable to an SCSI or other card in the computer. Such drives will vary widely in price based on capacity and format; expect to pay at least $1,000 for a decent array.

Your capture-card options will allow you to connect cameras and playback/record decks directly to your computer using higher-quality

Figure 2-17 *DeckLink HD Extreme capture card.*

cables than FireWire or USB. Typically, only professional cameras will offer these output options, so make sure your camera (such as the Panasonic AG-HVX200)0 offers this before buying a capture card. These cards will range from a few hundred dollars all the way up to several thousand, but they are well worth the expense if you're working in HD or any other high-end format. A popular card that can handle standard def and high def is the DeckLink HD Extreme (see Figure 2-17). Two great places for additional research, or if you're interested in pricing out turnkey systems, are DV.com and ProMax.com. The first site offers a wealth of knowledge on the constantly changing field of technology. Just about all editing is digital nowadays, so as an excellent guideline always remember Moore's Law: technology doubles every 18 months.[1]

---

[1] Although this is the common interpretation of Moore's Law, the actual law stated in 1965 by Intel co-founder Gordon Moore said that the number of transistors on a chip doubles about every two years.

Deciding to Rent or Buy?

Okay, so you've chosen what camera you want to shoot on, what mics you want to record with, what mounts you're going to use, and what system you want to edit on. Now you need to decide if it's worth buying all this equipment or just renting.

Even if you own some gear already, you can always rent your accessories to complement your camera, or even just try out a new camera you're considering buying. Like the demo shop at a ski resort, there is a lot of stuff to try and plenty of places to rent it. If you don't live near a big city, try calling a local production company and asking if they rent gear, or have them refer you to a rental house.

If you are shooting for a living and think you'll be making back the cost of purchasing your new gear within the first year, then I always think it's worth the investment. Remember, you can always charge an equipment-rental fee on top of your usual fee even after you've paid off your gear. On the other hand, if you just shoot for fun or don't think you'll be able to pay off the purchase in a short time, then renting is always a safe option.

When I got into production in the mid-'90s, I began trying to accrue as much stuff as I could. But in the past ten years alone, the technology behind formats and quality has been changing so rapidly that I've been opting to rent most high-end gear, and purchase only less-expensive cameras and editing equipment. The devices I use on a regular basis — a Final Cut Pro HD bay, a Panasonic AG-DVX100A and AG-HVX200, a Sennheiser shotgun mic, and so on — I own. The higher-end HD and film cameras and fully uncompressed 10- and 12-bit HD edit and graphics bays, I opt to rent.

Project Development (a.k.a. Preproduction)

Having a Clear Goal

Many things in this world are universal. Most successful companies have a strong and clear business plan, most great Hollywood scripts start as well-plotted outlines, and almost all great shoots begin with a clear goal.

The concept is simple: know what you're going to shoot — or at least what you hope to shoot — before leaving the office or house. I find that although storyboards and scripts may be overkill for many simple shoots, a shot list in outline form of what I intend to capture usually makes a significant difference. Once you arrive at your location and begin shooting, whether it's a full-blown action-sports commercial or just shooting a contest for fun, it's very easy to eventually get caught up in the moment and miss, or forget, to capture a key shot.

To avoid missing shots, take a few simple steps. First off, for large events, bring a list of athletes you plan to cover. Then, as you go through the list, simply check off the names with two marks throughout the day: one mark for B roll of them riding, and one mark for a sound bite or lifestyle shot. In the event of commercials and scripted shoots, always keep a shot list in your back pocket, and constantly review it to make sure you're not only getting everything, but that you're also shooting things in the most efficient order. This may all sound like overkill if you're just making a skate video, but nothing's more frustrating than getting into the edit bay and realizing you don't have a close-up shot of your main athlete's face.

There's no production like preproduction. Every great project will begin in prep. Like the old days of shooting film prior to video, the more prepared you are going into your gig, the better off you'll be, and the better it will be. After all, the ultimate goal of most action-sports film-makers is to produce a piece that is both compelling and entertaining to your audience.

Illustration 3-1
Finding funding: Don't movies cost millions of dollars to make?

Okay, it's true most movies can cost hundreds of thousands — or even millions — of dollars to make. But in the words of Steve Martin in *Bowfinger:* "That's after gross net deduction profit percentage deferment 10 percent of the nut. Cash, every movie costs $2,184."

There are several types of financing available for your project, but they all follow one basic guideline: willingness to finance is directly proportionate to how many viewers you will get. Think of your work as a commercial; the more eyeballs you get, the more valuable it is. Therefore, if you know you'll be featuring top-name athletes or have a compelling untold story, it'll be easier to get someone to give you money. Investors expect to make their money back on a project, so when you pitch it, take an angle of how popular your film will be and why. Show a potential investor how similar projects in the past have done, and what will make your project unique (read more on this in Chapter 10, Distribution). Below are the basic financing options you'll encounter. For additional material, check out books such as *Filmmakers and Financing* by Louise Levison.

From government grants and tax incentives to debt financing and self-financing, you'll find that with a little research, there are real-world options to get your project paid for. Many state governments and even the federal government offer tax breaks and grants for certain types of films. However, there is always a limited amount of money allotted each year, so it's crucial to submit your project before that funding runs out.

The biggest obstacle to finding government funding through grants or taxes will be meeting the requirements they impose. If you plan to document a great athlete who was raised in Pennsylvania, for example, then you might be able to promote the beauty of the countryside in your film. This, in turn, can bring employment and tourism to Pennsylvania, and thus make it easier to get state funding for your project. The rules are different for every region, so read up online first, and then try your local film commission for more details.

The next option is debt financing. This can be the hardest for a small project because it involves selling the rights to distribute your work before you even make it. Similar to government financing, this option relies solely on the expected draw of your project. If, for example, you plan to feature five top-name athletes in your film, and the most recent video they were in sold 50,000 copies each, then you may be able to presell your project to distributors based on the estimated profit they think they will make. I recently had lunch with an up-and-coming director of independent films. Her project was coming up short on financing. She needed $3 million to make her movie, but the distributors were offering only $2.5 million for the project with the current actors attached. The result was that she now had to either cut out key elements of the film, which would hurt it in the long run, or replace her cast with a new actor who was "worth" more to the distributors/financiers. In Hollywood, this is a typical example of how debt financing can work.

Another option for action-sports videos is to sell off sponsorship rights to help get your film made. Sponsorship deals will usually be sent out with various options — for example, a gold, silver, or bronze package, each one involving a different level of financial or material commitment to related companies (see Table 3-1). Just like debt financing, if you are certain your film will get many viewers, then the advertising value is great to these potential sponsors, and getting them to help pay for your production is very possible.

One of the first skate videos I ever made was pieced together with deals like this. I wasn't able to get many companies to give me cash for the video, probably because it was my first, but they were willing to pay all my expenses to travel with their teams and document them on the road. I spent weeks overseas shooting the athletes on the sponsors' dime, in exchange for gold sponsorship packages on my video. The result was a very international feel with enormous talent in the video and very little overhead for me. Additionally, using the leverage I now had of guaranteeing the grand scope of the video, I worked in several promotional deals. One was with the then-booming Soap grind shoes. The company gave me 1,000 free sneaker vouchers to slip into the videos. In our ads, we promoted the chance to get the free shoes. I also traded ad space with several magazines, offering them a commercial in our video in exchange for a small ad in their magazine. When all was said and done, the project cost me very little beyond my time and energy, and ended up doing fairly well. Of course, I was just happy to have gotten my first video made.

Classify Your Project

To begin with, let's separate the types of projects into four main categories: documentary, commercial, short subject, and feature length. The most popular is the documentary, and will include the average 30- to 45-minute skate or other action-sports video, as well as the true-to-form

Table 3-1

Sample sponsorship packages	Cost ($)	Logo and name placement on all print and video	Secondary benefit
Gold	10,000	"*Your Name* Presents" top/front billing	Company athlete profile section
Silver	2,000	"Support from *Your Name*" lower/front	Company athletes in montages
Bronze	750	"Support from *Your Name*" bottom billing	N/A

Note: This represents structurally how an action-sports video-sponsorship deal could be done.

introspective interview-driven documentary. These videos exist in a wide range of sports, as seen in Table 3-2.

Short-subject videos are becoming more popular every day with the proliferation of the Internet and such sites as YouTube.com, MySpace.com, PureVideo.com, and now countless other sites that are not only sharing content but also profits with the project producers. One of the original profit-sharing sites, Metacafe.com, paid out well over $25,000 to a video producer for his clips of gymnastics stunt routines. These sites represent the first step toward the future of entertainment, and quite literally the changing era of the old distribution model.

It's always important to classify your project clearly and to know your end goal so you can best shape and mold it to the right audience. If your intention is to make a documentary on one popular action sport, then research what else is out there, and watch some of the most popular videos to get a better feel for what has worked in the past. Many ideas in these industries have been done, and then repeated, because content

Table 3-2

Sport	Popular Videos
Skateboarding	*411VM* video magazine, *Almost Round Three, Yeah Right!*
In-line skating	*VG* video magazine, *Barely Dead*
Surfing	*Riding Giants, Sacre Bleu*
Moto-X	*Crusty Demons of Dirt* series, *Nitro Circus* series
Snowboarding	Mack Dawg Productions, Defective Films
Skiing	Warren Miller Entertainment, *Corduroy* (Rage Films)
Wakeboarding	*Encore, DWP*
BMX	*Props* video magazine

producers didn't do their homework and check out prior works. As a former athlete myself, I can think of countless times when various film and TV producers, as well as documentarians and inventors, approached my friends and me with pitches and concepts that all started out the same: "We're gonna do this amazing thing — it's never been done." Of course, it already *had* been done. Keeping all this in mind, just go with your gut at the end of the day. If you think something similar to your project has been done, but you're really passionate about it, then perhaps it's still worth pursuing.

Passion . . . and Why You Need to Have It

If life is about passion, and work is about money, then what happens when you love what you do for a living?

It was 1999, and I was standing on top of a vert ramp somewhere outside of Los Angeles, filming the finals of a pro skate contest for ASA Entertainment. The weather was perfect, the skating was going off, and I was flying back and forth on the deck, shooting trick after trick, so

Figure 3-1 *C-17 shoot at 8,000 feet for USAF DoSomethingAmazing .com.*

excited and into it that I didn't notice or care who was watching me. As the contest wound down, another cameraman approached and said that someone in the crowd wanted to speak with me. I headed down the ramp, a little unsure of what to expect. The woman I met told me that she was an executive assistant at Warner Bros., and explained that my passion and excitement for what I was doing made it more entertaining to watch me than the competition. She handed me her office number on a napkin and said to stay in touch. Her name was CJ, and sure enough, she became a great friend and personal contact, getting my action-sports shooting and directing reel into the hands of several project-development executives who ended up meeting with me. She was one of the true blessings in my early years in Los Angeles.

Figure 3-2 *Neal Hendrix, fakie hurricane, shot from the deck at Camp Woodward. Photo by Bart Jones.*

The lesson learned here is that passion can be far more powerful than any other motivator. Nobody wants to get involved with a project whose founder doesn't even believe in it. If you pursue what you love, and ultimately do what you love, eventually you will find success, and the money for doing it will come as a by-product. Just keep your focus, keep yourself motivated, and keep your passion.

Choosing Talent and Getting a Release

Talent can be defined in many ways. Although it is most commonly used to describe ability levels, in the production world, the "talent" is simply the people you intend to shoot. If you are documenting a skate contest, then your talent is probably the competitors. If you're shooting a home movie, then your talent might be your friends or family. It all starts with the talent, and it's important to decide who best fits your project. Many great movies have horrible scripts or even terrible directing, but if you put the right cast in a story it always seems to work out. Take Johnny Depp, for example — the guy can't seem to make a bad movie.

Once you know the talent you will shoot, getting all the necessary releases is your next important step. If you plan to shoot a live event that's already been scheduled, you'll have to contact the event producers in advance and ask if you need a media badge or pass. Most events ask all athletes to sign waivers that include their photographic release. In this case, if the event organizer is okay with your being there shooting, then you may not need any further release from the talent. I strongly recommend that you review the release if you plan to distribute your project. Although most events do blanket all media for all uses as a way to get exposure for themselves, the last thing you want is to get a "cease and desist" in the mail for a video you spent a year creating.

Releases can be tricky as well. I've shot hundreds of events. Many times, athletes are happy to sign additional releases, so long as they understand how you plan to use the footage. The problem arises when you get your own release for an athlete, but you're shooting at some company's event. For example, the X Games try to maintain a healthy degree of control over their actual competition footage. I recently included some X Games shots, which I had done for them, on my camera work reel. I had posted my reel for some coworkers to see on YouTube, and the content got flagged and removed by ESPN. This is a bizarre example, considering that the footage was my own footage, and ESPN had hired me to shoot it — but it represents just how important getting proper clearance can be when you're dealing with a large company.

Figure 3-3 *Vans Cup at Tahoe, 2007. Courtesy Windowseat Pictures.*

If you plan to shoot athletes outside of an event, you'll usually have more time with them to prep. Being able to cruise into the city or to a local ramp will allow you to focus and work with them on what you need to get. From a release standpoint, you'll likely want to take care of any documents you have in advance. Get the paperwork out of the way, and keep it simple and unobtrusive. The last thing you want is to hand an athlete a thick, intimidating document that they're afraid to sign. Basic photographic and likeness releases can be found online, although you should talk to a lawyer about what you plan to do. I generally like to also include a paragraph that helps protect myself: a release of liability in case the athlete gets injured. A basic document can be as short as half a page, or as long as several pages.

Next, finding your talent can be difficult. If you have an idea for a project, you can always contact an athlete via the Internet by either finding their email address or discovering if they have a manager who represents them. There are a few companies that handle athlete management, and you might be able to work a deal to "package" a group of their clients for your project. Going through an agent or manager can be expensive and difficult, though. If you have any kind of connection through friends, that's always the best way to go. Talking to an athlete via someone you know, or even directly with the person yourself, will save you a great deal of time and energy. Athlete representatives get paid to manage and look out for their clients' careers; oftentimes they won't be too interested in a project if it's unpaid or a low-profile gig. That doesn't mean the athlete won't be interested, however; so if you can, always try asking them personally.

Insurance . . . Do you need it?

From shooting remote snowboarding in the Alps to capturing your buddies hitting handrails downtown, many projects happen without insurance. This is a sticky area, but there's a good rule of thumb to follow: if you aren't sure if you need it, ask a lawyer. Okay, so that was more of a disclaimer than a rule of thumb, but here are a few examples of what projects in the past have done.

Figure 3-4 A snow-boarder spins the big kicker at Northstar at Tahoe. Courtesy Windowseat Pictures.

First off, although insurance is crucial on many large productions, most action-sports home-video shoots happen without personal or production insurance. Being that most videos don't have large budgets, and most of the athletes and filmmakers should have their own health insurance, it oftentimes just isn't cost-effective to get a big-production insurance policy for a small video. Top action-sports videos are essentially documentaries, so the logic is that you are simply capturing athletes doing what they would have done anyway. Then again, this is America, and ever since McDonald's was sued for the hot coffee that some woman spilled on herself, I've been a little wary of logic. If you know the people you are filming — and trust them as well — then it's often a given that you don't have to worry about your personal liability. However, if you are serious about documenting a group of athletes for your video project, then a liability release, as mentioned earlier in this chapter, can be a good start.

Production insurance can cover your equipment, which is always an asset. There's nothing worse than shiny new gear getting destroyed because you got too close to the action. Once, while riding a motorcycle on an L.A. freeway, the wind pulled open a zipped backpack and sucked a microphone out of it.

If you have an apartment, a viable option is renter's insurance with a rider for electronic equipment. The rider should cover a realistic portion of your gear when you are working away from home. This way, if your camera gets jacked, you're covered. You can also opt for a credit card that has additional insurance options on products purchased with the card.

Illustration 3-2
Liability is always a concern.

If you're shooting a larger production that is less documentary and more scripted or cast, then you can be liable for the talent and equipment you buy or rent. You should therefore consider a full insurance policy. Depending on the insurance company you choose, your deductible, and other variables, a normal $1 million policy can run anywhere from $100 to $2,000 a day. This is the type of policy that many rental houses will require if you want to rent high-end equipment such as film or full-HD cameras. A good source of information can be found on the web at sites such as the Independent Feature Project (www.IFP.org).

If you plan on shooting and producing your piece alone, then doing your liability-coverage homework could certainly cover you later. If you are shooting a larger project and plan to hire a crew, then your line producer should be able to research the best option for you. Although many commercials for television are still shot with large crews, most action-sports home videos, Internet commercials, webisodes, and documentaries are shot alone or with a select few professionals. A person who produces and edits nowadays is sometimes referred to as a "predator." This means you're covering almost all aspects of the production alone, and if it's not scripted, then the producer is the closest thing to a director on the project.

Figure 3-5 Shooting/producing/editing — the action-sports championships trixionary.

Editors Make the Best Directors

There's an old saying that editors make the best directors. This is true not only for making the best directors, but also the best cameramen or producers. It's important for two reasons. First of all, as an editor, you get to see a wide range of work by various cameramen and directors. You can learn from their mistakes, be influenced by their style — and perhaps most importantly, get an overall sample of what has come before you. I remember cutting a short film for a college friend once, and going through the footage over and over again, looking for an insert shot to cut between two different takes from the same scene. Although it probably would have taken only a few minutes to shoot an insert, it never happened on the day,[1] and now his film was limited by what we actually had to work with.

You'll gain a lot from watching raw footage. People often ask how they can get better at shooting. In reply, the first question I ask them is if they really sit down and watch what they shot. To improve your shooting, the fastest way is to constantly review and critique your own footage. Sit in the edit bay and watch your work thoroughly. Think about what could have been better, what's missing, and what you can do next time to make sure you notch it up a little.

The second reason editors make great cameramen and directors goes back to the Indiana Jones scenario as described in Chapter 2. Editors are able to see how rough and raw footage can start out versus how polished and refined it appears when it's done. The process of cutting shots together, then adding visual effects, sound effects, music, and finally polishing it all can create a truly seamless piece that audiences will always get caught up in. So as an editor, you have the rare chance to truly see the potential and result of what was shot on the day.

As seen in the image in Figure 3-6, green screen can provide a very creative backdrop for taking a shot to another level. A great example

---

[1] "On the day" is a commonly used phrase to represent the period during which a shoot took place.

Figure 3-6 *On the set with Windowseat Pictures for a Vans commercial.*

of this can also be seen in the Girl and Chocolate skate company owner and legendary director Spike Jonze's *(Being John Malkovich)* skate video *Yeah Right!* Shooting the pro-team riders performing countless tricks on all-green skateboard setups allowed Spike to remove the skateboards in post and create an insanely unique section for the video. A little work and planning in preproduction was all it took to come up with and prepare the video section for what it was, groundbreaking. So don't be afraid to think outside the box. If you're going for a widely accepted video, keep a strong eye on what's accepted in the industry and what is perceived as cool — but beyond that, push the boundaries, get creative, and shoot what you are truly passionate about.

Working on Location

Safety

You can shoot in the safety of your neighborhood, you can shoot on soundstages or at production offices, but the moment you step outside and into the world, the parameters always change. One of the greatest things about action sports is their ability to creatively overcome obstacles in the real world by turning architecture and other man-made objects into the ultimate playground. The downside is twofold. First, this ability often winds up taking the athletes into more-dangerous parts of the city to session that perfect rail or hit up an amazing ledge. The second problem is that most high-end buildings — such as banks and museums, which often have incredible architecture — are open during the day, leaving nights and weekends as ideal times to session them. If you're traveling around a city at night or even on a Saturday in a less-than-appealing part of town, keep a real close eye on your gear. Although most athletes don't invite crime and are often very street-smart themselves, you still may be carrying anywhere from $3,000 to $10,000 in equipment with you, which is rather inviting.

In 2000, a photographer and good friend named Chris Mitchell was road-tripping through Las Vegas, shooting stills of a group of skaters alongside a videographer. After shooting all day, they returned to their small hotel just off the Strip to rest and make evening plans. Someone must have been watching them during the day and then followed them back — because moments after Chris and the videographer had settled into their room to download that day's shots, the door burst open and several armed and masked men entered. With guns pointed, these guys took most of the video- and still-camera gear and left. This is a rare thing to happen in any industry, but the bottom line is that it did — and could again. In a case like this, there may be little that could have been done to prevent the robbery; however, there are still things to be learned. Perhaps simple things, such as staying in larger hotels with security or utilizing more-discreet backpacks for gear. Either way, you can do only so much to protect yourself.

My advice is simple: when you hit the road, don't take all of your gear. If you think you may end up in questionable areas, pack light and bring only what you are likely to need. Nothing says "mess with me" like a brand-new HD camera with heaps of accessories and bags everywhere. As mentioned above, I always try to use low-key, subtle backpacks (see Figure 4-1). Earth tones, preferably black, are a great way to not advertise "camera inside" to a passersby.

Figure 4-1 *A perfect camera bag for on the road: the Ty Video 2 by Ogio.*

Figure 4-2 *A fully customizable interior.*

Airline Travel

When you hit the road with your gear, you may also encounter the potentially dangerous scenario of checking luggage, cameras, and tapes on airlines. My experience over the years has been that traveling with expensive gear is not a problem, so long as you have insurance. If you are flying into a location the day of a shoot and would have no time to rent or buy new gear, then carry your camera on the plane in a soft carry bag (see Figure 4-1) that will fit in the carry-on storage bin. If you must check it, don't check a soft bag. Instead, rent or purchase a hard case, such as a customizable Pelican Case, that can be locked and safely stowed in the plane's cargo hold as checked baggage. Online stores such as B&H Photo Video in New York City and Fry's Electronics will carry large Pelicans. The interiors of these cases are full of small removable foam blocks that you can tear out to make the perfect tight-fitting camera and accessory slots. The risk for checked luggage is that even cases can be stolen. I had a complete Sony three-chip camera package stolen once off the baggage-claim carousel at LAX coming home from a shoot, so be careful. Your only options to avoid being in the hole during travel are to carry insurance for your gear, get a production insurance policy for your shoot, or have a renter's insurance policy that covers gear when you're away.

If you're traveling home with tapes, then you may be concerned about the X-ray machines affecting your shot footage. In the old days, you could just ask for a hand check, but since 9-11, most airports will require that all material go through the machine. Sony and other companies have conducted extensive testing over the years with all types of DV, SD, HDV, and HD tapes, and found that no standard X-ray airport check-in machine will affect the magnetic tape. With FAA-enforced tightened airport security, there are now out-of-sight explosive-detection systems that incorporate far more powerful X-ray scanning for checked luggage. These systems are known to fog undeveloped, unexposed film. Although they're said not to affect magnetic tapes, I always prefer to carry mine versus checking them. If you do have undeveloped, exposed film, you can also consider separating your tapes and shipping them back using various trackable overnight shipments (more than one in case a shipment were to get lost). Just call and verify with the shipping company, though, because most overnight services use aircraft — they, too, may have X-ray scanning devices.

Cops and Security Guards: How to Deal with Them

There's one constant in the world of action sports, and that's the recurring issue with authority figures. The concern is justifiable when you consider that many great street spots are public areas that create liability issues. When bikes, skateboards, in-line skates, or other devices grind on rails and ledges that weren't meant to be used that way, damage does happen.

Some cops and security guards will simply ask you to leave the premises on the grounds that your sport isn't allowed. Others will tell you, especially in the United States, that liability is too big an issue, so you'll have to go. And finally, on rare occasions, you'll meet security officers who will be very cool about it and look the other way. I remember shooting a skate video in Europe once where I realized that the American obsession with liability is just that: an American obsession. We were sessioning a ledge down a set of stairs when a security guard came around the corner to talk to us. Instantly, half of the athletes I was with started to walk away; the other half of us stood our ground, basically cornered by the guard. He walked right up to us, and we figured he was about to kick us out. Instead, the guard said that he'd be in a booth right around the corner should anyone get hurt or need anything. We stood silent, confused by the response. Apparently, there are countries in which people support the popular activities of their youth, and the adults don't sue one another for their kids' accidents. Accidents happen — that's life.

Unfortunately, you'll be hard pressed to find a security guard like that in the United States, so you're going to need to take on a new approach in any U.S. shooting locations. Believe it or not, I actually know skaters who used to get kicked out of skate spots — and they're now grown up, married, and work as security guards. The bottom line is this: there are some cops and security guards who are actually cool and are even fans of action sports. So when someone they might otherwise respect comes at them with attitude and disrespect, of course they're going to kick that person out. After thousands of experiences and years and years of shooting and skating urban spots, I've found that a lot of the time, if you stop and hear out the guards, then talk to them with respect, they're more likely either to be cool about letting you stay, or at least take off and essentially give you free range at your next skate spot.

Rolling with the Punches

Studios are highly controlled environments. From the sets to the lighting to even the weather, you almost always know what you're getting. It's

Illustration 4-1 *Busted by security.*

on location that things can — and often will — change so frequently that your shooting needs to be as creative as the athletes themselves. When you're filming out on the streets, you can't always control what will happen next, which can be part of the adventure. From that last-minute thunderstorm to the crazy guy on the park bench who offers up words of wisdom to your talent, it's paramount that you always be ready to go. When I'm shooting documentary style, I keep the camera in my hand, turned on, and with my finger just a flick away from that red button. It's crucial to be ready to roll if something starts to happen. Sometimes you don't know how someone will react at first, and you may even want to start shooting subtly. Then, afterward, ask for their permission to use what you've recorded. Some great advice I was once given is that sometimes it's easier to ask forgiveness than permission.

Another big variable is the weather. I try to check the forecast and either bring a rain cover for my camera or improvise with a plastic shopping bag. Even the slightest bit of moisture will wreak havoc with the electronics, so keep your gear dry. If you've ever shot in extreme cold, then you also know this can shut your camera down. They may not be flesh and bone, but cameras will get glitchy and eventually seize up if they get too cold. PortaBrace (see Figure 4-3) makes cold-weather gear that actually has internal compartments for hand-warmer packets (like ones you'd use on a ski mountain). If you're shooting in the snow, or even just on a cold night, you'll need the warmth. I shot nights once in Prague in the winter, while making a documentary on the Vin Diesel film *xXx*, and my Sony DSR-PD170 was tough, but nothing could take that cold. Despite wearing two heavy jackets and wrapping the camera tight in a PortaBrace Polar Mitten, the cold was still piercing.

If you don't have the money to buy cold-weather gear, then a great makeshift option involves two plastic bags, some hand warmers, and, of course, duct tape. Start by inserting a few warming packets inside the first bag and taping each packet to the sides of the bag. Be sure not to cover the packets in tape, or the heat won't radiate. Next, put the second bag in the first one so it lines the insides, then tape them together. This will put the heater packets between the two bags, and create a warm layer of insulation (just like the wall of a house). This will also prevent your camera and hands from being exposed to the direct contact of the heaters, which can cause burns. Now cut a hole in the bottom of the bags just large enough for your lens to fit through. Tape the bag to the end of your lens to make sure that it won't move or get in the shot. This is also a seal to help keep the warmth in and the cold out. Finally, pull the bag over and down, covering the camera and leaving access to the controls through the back, via the main opening in the bag. If it's incredibly cold out, you can even double-layer the outer wall of the bag and then seal up the main opening around your wrist; but remember that you'll likely want to be able to get your second hand in and out regularly for accessing most of your manual settings. The end result may not look like much, but it should keep your gear functioning and your exposed hand from getting frostbite.

Protecting Yourself

There are plenty of things to jump out and ruin your day while shooting on location. All too often, we focus solely on the normal dangers at

Figure 4-3 *Polar Mitten cold-weather case by PortaBrace. Photo by Jasin Boland.*

hand: protecting the camera, watching the ground you're shooting from, and so on. What gets left behind are the not-so-standard dangers, the typical things that you take for granted every day because your attention is distracted by your shoot. In this case, I'm referring to such common mistakes as walking into the tail stabilizer of an F-14 Tomcat.

Figure 4-4 *Aircraft carrier USS* Nimitz.

In 2005, I was shooting somewhere off the coast of Mexico on the flight deck of the nuclear aircraft carrier the USS *Nimitz*. It was near the end of a two-year journey for a documentary I was making called *Harnessing Speed*, for director Rob Cohen's film *Stealth*. We were shooting night two, around 3 a.m., and no one had slept the first day because of the noise of fighter jets catching trip wires and being catapulted off. The film crew set up an incredibly visual rain scene with massive pipes and hoses on the carrier deck surrounding the fighter jets. The lighting and view of the moonlit Pacific Ocean were incredible, so I decided to drop the Sony HDR-FX1 HDV camera I was shooting with and go grab the full-HD camera I had in my bunk belowdecks, a Sony HDC-750A. I hurried past several parked F-14s and onto the catwalk that surrounds the railingless flight deck, some 70 feet above the cold, black ocean. As I was returning, rushing to get the shot, I ran up the catwalk steps to the flight deck, watching my footing carefully — and not noticing that I was quickly approaching the rock-hard tail section just above me. With camera and gear in hand, and no helmet on, I walked headfirst up and into the tail stabilizer of an F-14 Tomcat.

Figure 4-5 *The morning after my run-in with an F-14.*

This was, of course, a random occurrence that happened in an anything but common environment. But the lesson learned is that no matter where you are, there are always going to be things that will jump out at you. No matter how comfortable you get, shooting anything can be dangerous. If you add to that a dangerous environment, the potential problems can compound very quickly.

Shooting with Other Cameramen

Many action-sports cinematographers and cameramen will tell you that their goal is always to get the best shot. Unfortunately, if you shoot at events where other operators are going to be, then you sometimes have to settle for working around and/or with them.

There are times, such as when you're hired by the event company itself, that you may actually have priority over where you want to shoot. If this is the case, then you should be respectful of the person you might need to ask to move. Introduce yourself first and find out whom they're shooting for, make sure you mention whom you're working for, then ask them politely if they wouldn't mind trading spots with you. If you get any resistance, you can either move on, try one more time to reemphasize how important it is to the event producers themselves, or, if necessary, simply tell them that you have to shoot from there. Just know that if you kick someone out of his or her spot, you may have lost an ally — and the action-sports industry is very, very small.

If you're shooting an event as a general media person, meaning you have no direct affiliation to the event, then you have no right kicking anyone out of anywhere, so you'll have to work with others. Oftentimes cameramen are looking mostly for particular athletes, not all of them, so if someone's in a spot you really want to shoot from, ask them if you can jump in to just shoot your athletes, then hop out when their athletes are approaching or taking a run. If the cameramen are shooting everyone, then ask if they wouldn't mind trading out a little; most operators are friendly because what goes around comes around.

Figure 4-6 *A crowded deck of cameras.*

If you're shooting on a ramp or street obstacle with a fish-eye, you're going to need to get close to the action. Again, if you have seniority over others, you should still be conscientious about how much you're getting in everyone's shot. There is a rule of common etiquette among cameramen that allows them to all work together (like living under the same roof). Most will be okay with your grabbing some fish-eye lens shots, but don't take advantage of it; get a few shots, then get out. Everyone wants some clean shots of athletes with no cameramen in front of their lens.

If you are on the deck of a ramp, shooting wide with others who are also wide, now comes a little tricky maneuvering. Let's say an athlete is grinding across the coping of the ramp from your right to left, but to your right is another cameraman. You can step farther out onto the coping than he is, and shoot around him (with the camera basically hanging out over the ramp) as the rider approaches you both. But now, as the athlete gets close, you are going to have to step back onto the

73

deck as you pan left, allowing the rider to pass you, but also allowing the other cameraman to match what you were doing, but on your right side. This technique is an often-unspoken switch that will happen on ramps and street courses. It'll allow both of you to get relatively clean shots of the tricks without seeing each other. It does, however, take a little practice, and it's always crucial that you never risk getting in the athlete's way, or distracting them, just so you can get a shot.

Figure 4-7 *Working the deck to get the shot: Vans Pro-Tec Pool Party.*

The Politics of the Industry

Skating and other action sports weren't always political; compared to other businesses and professional sports, they still aren't very political today. But when you're working with professional athletes, dealing with sponsors, and shooting large-scale events, it's hard to avoid at least some politics.

Most politics come from the increase of money in the industry. Athletes have an obligation to their sponsors to promote them, and you may be a conduit for doing that. When you're shooting interviews with athletes, consider that what they're doing for you is a favor, by taking time out of their day, just as you're doing them a favor by helping to promote. It's a two-way street, and you can go a step further by incorporating their sponsors in your shot. Also be mindful of your shot's background, on the chance that certain event banners may conflict with the sponsor that the athlete rides for. If this is the case, try framing up nonconflicting banners as a means to help out the athlete and the event sponsors who are also helping you.

If you decide to shoot a major competition such as the X Games, you're going to need to contact them well in advance and get a media pass. You may have seen event badges or bracelets on all participants, authorized media, and crew. Although pretty much all action sports will

Figure 4-8 *Various event media credentials.*

allow you to shoot home video from the stands where spectators sit, you're not likely to get the best angles or coverage from there. Before a big event will give you a media credential, they'll want to know whom you are shooting with and what for. Some televised competitions don't like their events showing up in skate videos, but they're okay with news and general publicity, so this may be a somewhat gray area that you'll have to research and work with or around.

So from the politics of shooting with other cameramen to working with the event producers to gain access, when you enter the professional world of action sports, there's some navigating to be done. But don't let it discourage you. At the end of the day, almost all athletes still ride because they love it, and this core value winds up being the point of the sword for competitions and shoots. Some action-sports athletes may have mainstream sponsors (American Express and Toyota, for example), but even these sponsors understand that their riders represent them only on the unspoken grounds that they can continue doing their sport freely and in their own way. When you turn pro in football and other conventional team sports, you enter a world of rules and often-uptight expectations presented by the Establishment. The relaxed form of self-expression that made action sports so popular in their infancy still reigns today — and hopefully, will always stay at the core of action sports.

Camera Angles, Lenses, and Framing

Up until now, we've discussed many general principles regarding the process of shooting action sports. This chapter will begin with many of the technical approaches — including lenses, angles, shots, and various tricks and tips — that will apply both in the field and on a set. There was a time when almost all action sports were shot by two distinct types of people, each with their own distinct style of shooting. The first was the action-sports participant or friend of a participant: usually a skater who just happened to love filming. In the early days of shooting, this person would go out with a video camera and a wide-angle lens — and nothing more. Almost all shots would be handheld, and very rarely would you see anything captured from any great distance. It was up close and personal, all the time.

The other type of videographer was the ENG-style shooter. ENG was a term coined by newscasters to reference the "electronic news gatherers" — the videographers of the late 1970s who would go out and document the world for the news. Today, ENG still refers to camera operators and shoulder-carried cameras. The first X Games and Gravity Games were shot almost entirely with ENG cameras and operators. This resulted in a very "high and wide" newscast feeling.

The ENG style of shooting was thought to be too stale and distant for the skaters, and yet the skater style of shooting was too rough and raw for professional cameramen. What came next — and what you likely see in many skate videos and on TV today — is a blend of these two styles. The idea is that both offer great assets to capturing action sports, and that operating with just one style isn't practical. Skate videos, commercials, and action-sports events now feature on-the-ground, handheld, DV, HDV, or HD operators who take time to grab ENG-styled shots that capture the big picture. Skate video makers will shoot artistic, creative shots through a fence or with other foreground elements. They'll do lock-offs, pans, and handheld all in the same section of the video. They'll even preplan their style of shooting based on what song they intend to use for that video section. And both of these styles of shooting begin with the same essential building blocks: five key framing sizes.

Figure 5-1 *Master shot.*

Figure **5-3** *Medium shot.*

Figure 5-4 *Close-up.*

Figure 5-5 *Extreme close-up.*

Each of these frames can be achieved with a wide range of goals in mind. Sometimes the use of the close-up will be for helping to tell your story. If you're shooting a snowboarder, and he's spinning a 540 off a kicker while nose-bonking a post, it may be helpful or just interesting to get a close-up (insert shot) of that nose bonk on another take. It's worth pointing out, however, that most core audience members (action-sports participants themselves) frown upon cutting to different angles in the middle of a trick. The logic being that, although you may think it makes the trick more exciting, cutting away is really doing two detrimental things. First, it's taking away from the ability to see and enjoy the move itself. Second, it's not actually showing that they did the stunt all the way through and landed it. Keep in mind that almost all action sports are progressive, and feature riders doing moves that nobody has done before. The problem occurs in highly technical or extremely difficult tricks, where it might be possible to cut together what looks like an athlete pulling off a stunt — when, in fact, they may not have done it. One way around this is to show the bulk of the trick after your insert or close-up, or simply to show it twice if it's amazing: once in the wide master shot, then once in the close-up. Any stunt that is likely to be questionable as to whether someone did it or not will usually be worth seeing it twice.

Figure 5-6 A silhouette at the YMCA in Escondido, California. Photo by Ryan Jordan.

The goal of your close-up could be to demonstrate the trick and clearly show its technicality. In addition, your close-up can also provide a cool artistic angle that can look very impressive. I find it's always wise to grab your master or wide shot first, though, just to make sure you have one solid take in the can before moving on to more difficult ones. Because many difficult tricks can take a few tries to land, or at least to get them smooth, then shooting the wide master first will provide a second angle for you where any small mistakes or bobbles will be less noticeable to the camera.

While recently shooting a pro skateboarder doing a very technical vert trick for a how-to section, I decided to start by getting all of the wide and distant angles that would emphasize how he takes off, but not clearly show how he lands. That's because I knew it would take him many tries to get it. I figured once I got the wide shots and obscure takeoff angles, I could move in for the hero shots that would feature the trick up close and highlight his landing. This kept the camera pressure off him for practicing, and made the shoot more efficient for me at the same time. Almost no shot went to waste in the final edit.

The same applies for acting: start wide, let everyone get comfortable with the scene and their lines (like an athlete with their trick), then slowly move in to a medium shot, and finally, a close-up. Just remember: the tighter you get on your subject, the more difficult it is to pan and tilt with them, keeping them in your frame.

The idea of shooting like a cameraman, and not a camera operator (as discussed in the preface), will come in handy here. By keeping your second eye open, you'll be able to see where the athlete is headed and what is about to come into your tight frame. This will help you to judge and predict what's going to happen next, which is especially helpful when shooting close-ups.

Prime vs. Zoom Lens

A lens is any device that bends light, causing it to converge and focus on a point smaller than the one it came from, or causing light to diverge and spread to a wider point. From the earliest known use of a lens (424 BC, when someone in a Greek play used a small device to focus the sun's light to start a fire), all the way up to modern contact lenses and telescopes, all of these lenses are fundamentally the same as what you'll find in your camera.

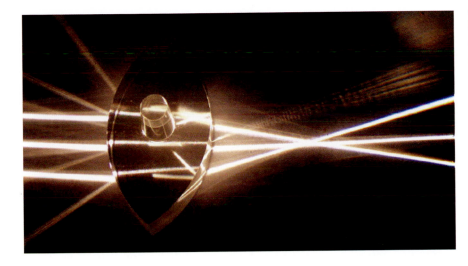

Figure 5-7 *A simple lens focusing light. Courtesy Wikimedia Commons.*

As a general rule, pretty much all of the shots discussed so far can be achieved with most standard video-camera lenses. The majority of consumer and prosumer cameras will have the ability to attach additional lenses, but very few will actually let you swap out the lens that came with the camera.

Aftermarket lenses for your camera will come in two main types: primes and zooms. A prime lens is essentially one of fixed focal length[1] — be it wide or telephoto, it cannot change. These are usually far better lenses — the glass is of higher quality, and there are fewer moving parts. Another benefit of prime lenses is that they often allow much lower f-stops (for more info, see F-Stop and Aperture, later in this

---

[1] The focal length is the distance from the focal point of a lens to the surface onto which it is focusing the light. This distance changes in most video cameras as you zoom in and out.

Table 5-1

Interchangeable-lens cameras	Fixed-lens cameras (DV and HD)	
Canon XL H1	Sony HDR-FX1 & FX7	Canon GL2
Canon XL2	Canon XH A1 & XH G1	Panasonic AG-HVX200
JVC GY-HD110U & HD200U	JVC GR-HD1	Panasonic AG-DVX100B
Panasonic AG-HPX500	Sony HVR-A1U, V1U, & Z1U	Sony DCR-VX2100

Note: Select prosumer cameras only.

chapter), which will allow you to achieve a shallower depth of field (for more info, see Depth of Field, later in this chapter), as well as to shoot in lower lighting. A zoom lens, however, will let you adjust its focal length in varying degrees, just like the internal lens of most video cameras. The problem arises when you begin to zoom through your internal lens, and a common fringing of color and light called chromatic aberration occurs around the image (see Figure 5-8). This is sometimes only slightly visible on consumer cameras; you may not even notice it. However, if the shot requires that pristine clean image, and you don't need to zoom, then additional lenses can provide a much nicer image by leaving your fixed lens at its widest point.

Long Lens vs. Fish-Eye

When it comes time to choose your zoom or prime lenses, you'll have two principal types to pick from: wide lenses (including fish-eyes) and long lenses (also called telephotos). Let's start by discussing the difference in lens language between film and video cameras. Film-camera lenses are typically measured in millimeters, just like an SLR (single-lens

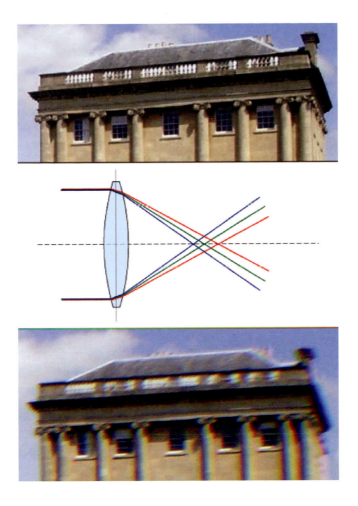

Figure 5-8 *An example of chromatic aberration.*

reflex) still-photography camera. A standard film-camera lens is a 35 mm, compared to a 50 mm lens on an SLR; these are very similar to what the human eye sees. The lower you go, the wider it gets; the higher the number, the longer it gets (or more telephoto). Although the millimeter sizes do differ by the type of camera (for example, a 16 mm film camera with a 50 mm lens will not be the exact same frame size as a 35 mm film camera with a 50 mm lens), on average, any camera with a lens reaching down to the low teens or even single-digit millimeters will be a very wide angled lens, eventually becoming a fish-eye. On the contrary, a 100 mm lens and higher will be a fairly long lens. Extremely long lens shots are often shot on lenses as long as 400 mm or even 800 mm. At this size lens, you'll need a very stable camera tripod and fluid head because every little movement will show up in your shot. If you're shooting something from a great distance, such as a snowboarder or skier descending the face of a mountain, you may be operating from a distant point with an incredible zoom lens, giving you the ability to get in tight on the athlete, then pull out to reveal the mountain face they are on. Some great examples of this are in the 2005 snowboarding film *First Descent*.

By using various adapters, almost all of the mentioned lenses can be attached to most video cameras. In fact, many high-end DV, HDV, and HD shoots can be done using Panavision[2] prime and zoom lenses. These lenses are the cream of the crop, and are best known for their glass (even on a video camera, you'll see the quality difference by using high-end glass from Panavision). Renting an adapter for these lenses and then a whole lens package can be expensive. More often than not, action sports are shot with basic made-for-video lenses. For these lenses, the measurements are slightly different from those of a film-camera lens. Instead of measuring in millimeters, they have a 0-and-up decimal system. By this standard, a 1.0X is the center point of normal for the human eye. The higher you go, the more telephoto the lens becomes — a 2.0X lens being twice as telephoto as the standard lens (similar to a doubler on most ENG-style video-camera lenses). Most telephoto lenses start at around a 1.5X, although I always feel that's too close to your standard lens. I usually opt for at least a 2.0X or higher (see Figure 5-9). Just keep in mind that most telephoto lenses won't give you a clean frame when you zoom all the way out; they'll vignette around the edges (see Figure 5-12).

Most video cameras with a fixed lens will prevent you from swapping it out for others, although you can always thread on or mount additional lenses to the front of the camera. Bayonet mounts are the easiest

---

[2] Panavision is a legendary motion picture production and equipment company providing the largest quantity of 35 mm film cameras and lenses to the entertainment industry.

to use, and offer the quickest and simplest attachment for gun-and-go shooting. Thread-on lenses can strip with time or simply take too long to attach if you are hurrying to get a shot off.

As you move into lenses below the standard 1.0X, the wider shots will allow you anywhere from very small increases in what you see, all the way up to a near-180-degree field of view. As you approach 0.5X lenses, the image will begin to slightly warp and distort on the edges, the telltale sign of the fish-eye lens. A great wide-angle lens that does not distort is a 0.7X lens (see Figure 5-10). It'll provide approximately 30 percent more image than your camera would get on its own, but doesn't add so much image as to be distracting. Another important feature of some wide-angle lenses is the ability to zoom through. Most low-end wide lenses aren't built to allow your camera to use its zoom while they're attached; the image will go out of focus, or

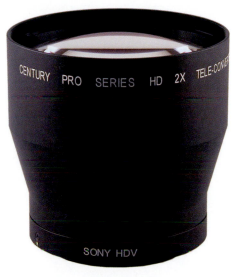

Figure 5-9 Thread-on 2X telephoto lens.

Figure 5-10 Bayonet-mount 0.7X wide-angle lens.

soft, the moment you push in. Century Optics (which now has merged with Schneider Optics) makes a phenomenal lens: a 0.7X wide-angle converter that allows you to zoom all the way through the lens while maintaining sharp focus. This lens provides superior image quality for its price (approximately $850) compared to most of the lenses I've used. Although I always travel with a telephoto and a fish-eye, the 0.7X is my standard go-to lens for capturing most action-sports events.

87

Figure 5-11 *Shooting the Vans Cup, Northstar at Tahoe, with the 0.7X wide-angle adapter. Courtesy Windowseat Pictures.*

When a lens takes in an extremely wide angle view, it is known as a fish-eye lens. Similar to lower-end wides and telephoto lenses, low-priced fish-eyes can also have issues. Many will begin to vignette[3] around the edges when you're at the widest (see Figure 5-12). There are, however, a few high-end lenses that should provide a virtually clean image with no vignette (see Figure 5-13). These lenses are so wide, and their glass element so broad, that the camera won't see the metal casing or frame that holds them. One issue to be cautious of is your steady shot. All cameras capture a slightly larger image than what you see in the viewfinder. Functions such as Sony's SteadyShot allow this larger image to "float" around as you shoot, helping to take any shaky movements out of what you're seeing. Because of this floating, the edges of

---

[3] Vignetting is a decreasing image brightness or clarity around the image's outer edges.

the true full image are approached, and if your fish-eye lens is vignetting just outside the normal frame, then, when SteadyShot is engaged, that black vignette will float into and out of your visible frame. To complicate the matter even more, keep in mind that televisions crop your image, which can mostly hide the edges of your frame, but the Internet does not; QuickTime video clips, for example, show the entire full frame. Any vignetting can be very distracting, so I try to always keep SteadyShot switched off while shooting with fish-eyes.

The fish-eye lens that the majority of the industry uses is the Century Optics 0.3X Ultra Fisheye Adapter. In the core action-sports photographic community, this lens is also referred to as the "death lens." Because of the extreme wide shot it allows, most operators end up getting so close to the action that the lens ultimately gets hit and "killed." The downside to this lens is its inability to zoom through (you can zoom in only about 25 percent before the image goes soft). However, the upside is massive. The fish-eye lens is so wide, providing a 130-degree horizontal field of view, that everything on the edge of the frame appears far away, and everything in the center appears exponentially closer. This results in a truly stylistic and cool image that plays extremely well with close-up action-sports shots. Athletes passing you will appear to whip by at high speed, close-ups on grinds will look so close it'll feel like you're there, and the warped outer frame will create a completely unique and exciting image.

Noting the street name of the death lens, it's only fair to warn you that if you aren't familiar with the camera, you should probably start by shooting at a safe distance from the action. The lens can get amazing shots within a few inches of the action, which puts you, your camera, the lens, and the athlete in danger — so be careful.

The most common technique for operating with this fish-eye is to use your LCD, and *not* the eyepiece. Because you cannot properly judge distance to your subject by looking solely through a lens that has the sole purpose of distorting distance, you'll need to keep your eyes on the subject, and then operate by "feel" (see Figure 5-15). This can take some practice to make sure you're framing the action accurately, but through trial, review, and additional trial, you'll nail it.

Figure 5-12 Vignetting as seen through a low-end fish-eye lens.

Figure 5-13 Century Optics 0.3X ultrawide-lens image. Courtesy ASA Entertainment.

Figure 5-14 No lens adapter used. Courtesy Todd Seligman.

Figure 5-15 Shooting action by feel. Courtesy ASA Entertainment.

The price of the Century Optics 0.3X lens can vary greatly by camera. For most standard DV and HDV cameras, you'll pay around $850 for a death lens, although the Panasonic AG-HVX200 death lens is quite a bit more. With a lens of this size and value, you'll also need to protect the front element.[4] Most of these lenses have a front and rear piece of glass, and any scratches or dings cannot easily, if at all, be buffed out. You can, however, replace a single element if it gets scratched, so don't sweat having to buy a whole new lens for most versions. Do your best to get the action up close, but not too close!

If you're not shooting with a standard DV or HDV camera, there aren't many options out there for high-quality fish-eye shots, but there is a simple trick worth mentioning. As cell-phone cameras become higher and higher quality, the ability to shoot a trick with your phone, and later edit it into a video, is becoming more and more realistic. It'll take some trial and error to find the appropriate distance for proper focus and avoid vignetting, but if you go down to the hardware store and purchase a short peephole for a door, you can attach it to your cell-phone camera lens and actually shoot fish-eye shots. Peepholes vary in focal width and shape, so bring your phone and try a few different models to find that perfect shot. Also bear in mind that when you get close to the action, it's going to be moving much more quickly, and if your camera is of lower quality (perhaps shooting only 15 frames per second versus the normal 30 fps), then a blurring effect will be severely accentuated.

F-Stop and Aperture

Your aperture is the round opening through which your camera allows light to enter. In the world of video and film, you can adjust your iris (which is the diameter of this opening) to control how much light enters. Your f-stop is a measurement of the diameter of your aperture (or iris). This measurement (also sometimes called the f-number, f-ratio, or focal

---

[4] The element of a lens is any one of the key glass components.

Figure 5-16 A cell-phone camera with a fish-eye attached.

ratio) is adjusted to compensate for the brightness of the image you're shooting. This is very similar to how your eye works when you walk outside into bright daylight. If you leave the camera on auto-iris, the aperture will close when the environment becomes brighter, and then open up if the camera needs more light in a darker environment.

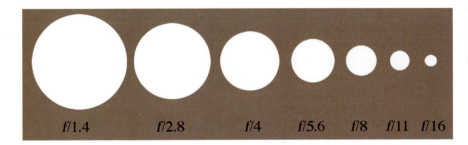

| f/1.4 | f/2.8 | f/4 | f/5.6 | f/8 | f/11 | f/16 |

Figure 5-17 Apertures/ f-stop diagram in single-stop increments.

These adjustments can also be made manually. I typically set my f-stop where I want it, then leave it for most of the shoot or until I notice the lighting beginning to change. Going to a lower f-stop number, perhaps from an f/5.6 to an f/2.8 (also known as opening up), will be used for dark interiors or night shoots. A higher f-stop, perhaps going from an f/5.6 to an f/11.0 (also known as closing down the iris), will be used for bright daylight. Several factors are affected by your f-stop. One of the most critical is your depth of field. What happens is that smaller stops, such as an f/2.8 (a very open aperture), will decrease your depth of field, allowing less of your shot to be in focus at the same time. Higher stops, such as an f/16.0 (a less open aperture), will conversely increase your depth of field, creating sharp-focus backgrounds.

So, for example, if you are shooting with the Century Optics 0.3X Ultra Fisheye Adapter mentioned above, you're likely going for the largest depth of field possible. By shooting with a higher f-stop number, such as a 16, you'll know you're getting more in focus. The only way, though, to open up the iris and shoot with such a high f-stop, especially if you're in broad daylight, will be to compensate with shutter speed or neutral-density (ND) filters. Otherwise, your shot will be overexposed (also called blown out). One example of this would be a low f-stop with a higher shutter speed or additional ND filters (more on this below). This is a good trick to help guarantee that your shot will be in focus, especially if you're operating by feel and not by the eyepiece.

There are times when you want to lessen your depth of field, even if you're shooting with the fish-eye lens. It's a good trick you can do when you get your first scratch on the lens and you can clearly see it in your shot, or if you're shooting in dust or rain and don't have time to keep cleaning your lens. This trick will lessen your depth of field—which can be a little risky, but it'll help get rid of that distraction on your lens. Try engaging a single or double ND filter, or simply increasing your shutter speed; now, to compensate for how dark the shot looks, open up the aperture to the smallest f-stop possible (say, an f/2.8). The result is that although you will still be able to find a narrower point of focus for your subject (just don't accidentally hit the focus ring while you're shooting), you will essentially be "pushing" that point of focus away from the camera. The farther away your depth of field is, the less in focus the front element of the lens itself will be; so that scratch or raindrop on the lens winds up going so out of focus it's hardly noticeable.

Figure 5-18 Richie Velasquez in a large depth of field created by a higher f-stop (f/16). Photo by Chris Mitchell.

Depth of Field

The depth of field is the portion of your shot that is perceived to be in focus. I say "perceived" because all shots will actually hold only one precise distance from the lens in focus, and then the surrounding area before and after that region will fall out of focus either slowly or sharply. In the case of the surrounding area slowly falling out of focus, this creates a large depth of field in which the vast majority of your shot will appear in focus.

Figure 5-19 A shallow depth of field created by a lower f-stop (f/2.8).

Figure 5-20 A long lens creates a very shallow depth of field of Shea Nyquist. Courtesy ASA Entertainment.

A key decision you'll make is whether you want your entire shot to be in focus or whether you want a more cinematic look — in which the background or foreground is out of focus, but your subject is sharp. This is the film look often used in movies, especially during close-up shots in which you can't even make out the background at all. As discussed in Chapter 2, cameras with a 24 p function will greatly increase that film-like feel. The second most common way to get the film look is to use the long end of your zoom lens while at a distance to your subject. By zooming in from a great distance, then opening your aperture up and increasing your shutter speed, you can cut your depth of field down to an absolute minimum. Your point of critical focus will become so small that much of the surrounding world will be out of focus. Although film cameras can achieve this look much more easily, it is possible on video cameras. This is one of my favorite long-lens shots because it can be used to create unique and artistic frames (see Figure 5-20).

If an athlete is grinding down a handrail from right to left, oftentimes a profile shot, from as far away as your lens will let you go, can create a very cinematic angle. You can even shoot through something close to you, such as a fence or tall grass, which will remain so out of focus it'll hardly register. This can help to create the illusion of speed, or to simply make a more compelling shot. Oftentimes in action sequences, directors will find any thin, tall, recurring obstacles to shoot through as they track alongside their subject. With these objects out of focus in the foreground flashing through the frame at high speed (called strafing), the shot will seem more intense. Think of it like this: when you drive in a car through the open country, the mountains or buildings way off in the distance appear to move very slowly, whereas the road and nearby objects whip past at high speed. This perceived difference in velocity can work for you when shooting. If you're tracking alongside a skater through a parking lot, try moving away from them, and shooting through a fence or parking meters if possible. As these objects begin strafing through your frame, you'll quickly see a change in the intensity and speed of the shot.

Another trick is to shoot athletes from the front or back as they are grinding a long curb on a street or the coping of a ramp. If you shoot

Figure 5-21 *Soft-focus foreground elements show a shallow depth of field. Courtesy ASA Entertainment.*

from far enough away, you can set your depth of field to be extremely shallow, and then rack[5] with the athlete as he or she grinds toward or away from you. Manipulating and controlling what you allow people to see will bring your filmmaking skills to an entirely new level. Whereas the average home videographer will simply point and shoot with their camera in hopes of capturing all of a scene or shot, the true professional will selectively choose what is revealed. Some of the most compelling scenes in the world don't show the entire environment they were shot in.

---

[5] Racking refers to adjusting the focus or zoom as you keep with or change the focus of your shot.

They leave it up to the imagination to fill in the rest. Consider Alfred Hitchcock's memorable shower scene in *Psycho* It was what we *didn't* see that made that scene — and Hitchcock's style — so legendary.

A final key element to understand with depth of field is hyperfocal distance. This refers to the nearest point to the camera in which you can hold focus, while keeping everything else in the distance in focus (to infinity). Every focal point will hold in focus more beyond it than before it. The focus of almost all lenses can be set to infinity so that everything off in the horizon appears in focus; just keep in mind that the hyperfocal distance is the point near the camera that's in focus when set to infinity. Let's say you're shooting down the mountain as a snowboarder is going off a jump. If you stay wide, there's a good chance your lens will maintain its hyperfocal distance close enough to you that the snowboarder will be in focus, along with that amazing mountain range on the horizon. On the other hand, if you do the opposite, you can head uphill as far away from the jump as possible, then zoom in on the kicker and focus there, likely throwing the distant mountains out of focus. Again, these are tools for you to use to better tell your story through selective composition.

Figure 5-22 *Athlete and horizon in focus with a larger depth of field. Photo by Dave Mead, Windowseat Pictures.*

Composition

Does your shot feel top-heavy? Is it too bright on the left side? Do you prefer to have only the lower right corner in focus? These are samples of the questions you need to ask yourself regarding composition.

Figure 5-23 *A two-shot is generally a well-balanced frame.*

Composition refers to the placement of elements, or how you frame those elements, within any given shot. If, for example, you choose to compose a shot of two subjects (see Figure 5-23), with one on each side of the frame (often called a two-shot), then your frame will likely be very well balanced. An important concept in composition is to decide first, if and when you want your frames balanced, and second, how you plan to achieve the feeling you want.

A common misunderstanding is that a well-balanced frame is the same thing as a symmetrical frame; for example, you could use a source of light in the lower left corner to balance out your main subject in the upper right. Although this frame is nowhere near symmetrical, it is balanced. An important rule of thumb in framing and composition is called the rule of thirds. This idea breaks your frame up evenly into thirds, vertically and horizontally, creating nine identically sized sections. According to the rule of thirds, you must keep your main subject or focus out of the center box. This rule helps to maximize the feeling of depth and scale in many shots, but it is only a guideline for shooting, not an actual rule.

Figure 5-24 *The rule of thirds keeps the subject off center. Photo by Chris Mitchell.*

An integral part of composition is also fad oriented. Just as the films and videos of our lives change and mature in style, so do trends in what's considered acceptable composition. Although there is no denying that a well-balanced frame feels nice, there are changes in what is popular with the public (similar to how fashion changes).

Years ago, many interviews for documentaries, television shows, and skate videos were framed with the subject closer to the center. Nowadays, it's considered not only acceptable, but even artistic, to frame your subject to an extreme side of your shot.

Figure 5-25 *A classic interview frame with Jon Julio. Courtesy Chris Mitchell.*

Figure 5-26 *2007 interview frame at Vans Cup Tahoe. Courtesy Windowseat Pictures.*

Also used to shape the composition of your frame are lighting and focus. Many great works of art and photographs were made with a specific point of focus in mind. This idea holds true in film and video as well; your audience's attention can be selectively focused on any part of your frame if you sculpt your shot appropriately.

If your goal is simply to achieve well-balanced frames and not make an artistic piece, then always keep in mind the concept of weight within each frame you shoot. Every object you shoot has a perceived feeling of weight. In filming, "weight" is often used to describe how strongly an image pulls the eye to it; think of this as actual gravity pulling your gaze in. If you frame something to the top of your shot but nowhere else, and don't plan to pan or tilt, then your frame will likely feel top-heavy. Likewise, if you put that eye-catching element elsewhere in your frame — be it a person, a bright light, or even an interesting building, all of which have weight — then it will subsequently pull the eyes of your viewers in that direction.

Unfortunately, the technique to maintain a balanced frame and avoid a left-heavy or other unbalanced frame has no mathematical formula. It's either a gut instinct (if you have it, people may always have said you have a "great eye" for photos or videos), or it's a learned trait that comes from studying great films and videos. Oftentimes, by just stopping and looking at your frame, you can tell if it doesn't feel right. Look at the image in Figure 5-27, then at the one in Figure 5-28, and see if you can "feel" the difference in how each is balanced.

As you can see in Figures 5-27 and 5-28, something as simple as an inanimate object in your frame can truly bring balance to it. There are no rules as to what you can use, but here are a few basic examples of what will work.

The key to all of these elements is to do what feels natural. Although most filmmakers and videographers will develop a bag of tricks containing their favorites, I'd recommend that you be open to all shots and techniques. Action sports and documentaries are usually unscripted, so you can't completely predict what you'll find and what might happen on your shoot.

Figure 5-27 A "left-heavy," or unbalanced, frame.

Figure 5-28 An upper right tree balances a would be left–heavy frame. Photo by Bart Jones.

Table 5-2

Building	Bright light	Distinctive color	Large object	Additional subject
Obstacle	Point of focus	Naturally occurring lines	On-set lighting	Postproduction lighting or color

Note: Various examples of what can be used to balance your frame.

Many times on many shoots, I've found myself in a location that appears flat and boring — or, worse yet, what I'm shooting doesn't appear as impressive as it is or should be. When this is the case, I quickly find a way to add layers to the shot through composition and the other techniques listed above. All of these tricks and methods will lead to better shots and a bigger bag of tricks for you as a shooter.

Shooting Techniques

Art vs. "In Your Face"

In 1995, the first year of the X Games, action sports were still extreme sports, and the all-too-common wide-angle-lens/in-your-face MTV approach of shooting seemed to make a lot of sense. But that was well over a decade ago. Since that time, photography has progressed a great deal, just as action sports have.

Many videographers out there think of themselves as so much more than just cameramen. They take pride in their own artistic style and approach to filming action sports. It is in this pride and creativity that a whole new breed of action filmmaking has been born.

When you begin to look at the frame of your shot as an extension of who you are, you'll find your personal style. Just as every great motion picture filmmaker has a distinct style of filmmaking, so can you. Whether you want to shoot grungy, in-your-face dramatic shots, or poetic, natural, artistic shots, it's entirely up to you. But I promise that you will find a great deal of satisfaction from learning and understanding both approaches.

Artistic shots usually have two goals: first, they find a way to maintain the focus on and respect for the athlete or trick being performed; second, they capture the environment in a unique and clever fashion. Artistic shots can include soft-focus use, foreground elements, background elements, and interesting composition, as discussed in Chapter 5. But they

Figure 6-1 An "at the lens" action shot, Vans Cup Tahoe. Photo by Dave Mead, Windowseat Pictures.

Figure 6-2 An artistic lock-off shot. Courtesy Chris Mitchell.

can go a step further from just using the in-camera settings and basic framing options that you have; they can come in large part from camera placement. By thinking outside the box when you arrive at a location, you might find interesting angles that speak to you or speak well of the location.

I was shooting by a subway stop outside San Juan, Puerto Rico, one summer, doing a road-trip section for a video. The goal of the segment was to capture the local flavor and emotion of the trip. We found a unique set of stairs with a handrail under a large concrete covering in which numerous homeless people were sleeping. A sad location to be in, but it was true; it was real. I framed some homeless dwellings on the left side of the scene, with the handrail on the right, all the while shooting through the bars of a fence. Now granted, you could have just looked at it and thought it felt like a cool shot, so why not do it? But more than that, the scene helped to tell the story of where we were, and emotionally what this part of town represented. The literal and metaphorical distance that shooting through the fence created was right in line with how we all felt about the unfortunate homeless plight of the area. The section wound up being edited with a good deal of slow motion and lifestyle footage to really encapsulate what we saw and where we were. In the end, the goal is to capture the best action-sports shots possible for your project, but if you can do it with a unique eye, then all the better.

Figure 6-3 *End-of-day surf in Maui, Hawaii. Photo by Dave Mead. Courtesy Windowseat Pictures.*

Shooting from a unique perspective and finding your style doesn't always happen overnight. Sometimes it can take years to find what feels right to you, to discover your visual signature. If you were shooting with a wide or fish-eye lens, then perhaps getting right under the trick and finding a crazy, up-close angle is what you want; or maybe a lock-off angle by the landing would look interesting; or perhaps you'll allow the athlete to do their trick, land, and roll out of frame without panning or trying to stay with them. If you're filming a session in a downtown urban area, then maybe try shooting from across the street, through passing cars. These interesting frames can add so much more to the footage and give your camerawork that unique style that'll make it stand out and start to truly become yours.

Followcam

Followcam is the act of tracking with and shooting your subject from behind, in front, or alongside, through any means of movement — usually a skateboard, snowboard, or in-line skates. In the film business, the technique is usually referred to as 'chasing' the subject and can be done from an ATV, modified camera car, or even by foot, using expensive but smooth Steadicam rigs. Major sporting events have adapted the technique through the use of cable and wire systems that suspend cameras over the sports venue. From football events to the X Games, cable rigs are used more and more often today. Even in film, this kind of technology has grown in popularity with high-end equipment made by Spydercam, a unique company with rigs that allow for almost any type of camera to travel at very high speed over roads, land, and buildings in any direction. A Spydercam setup is an amazing rig that is capable of some truly unique shots.

In action sports, the money for these kinds of systems isn't always available, nor is it always necessary. Although commercials often use the latest technology, the more grounded projects such as videos and documentaries find this equipment bulky, overpriced, and too intrusive.

The absolute most basic standard technique of shooting most action-sports projects is to simply follow the athlete on the same device they're riding. Many talented filmmakers who are great athletes themselves now shoot film and video for a living, so the followcam comes very naturally and easily.

The key to a solid followcam starts with these three things. First, know what you're doing. This sounds overly simple, but it's true. You need to be so comfortable on your wheels or board that the riding part comes naturally — and even then, remember how quickly your environment can jump up and bite. Half of your attention or more may be going to the shot you're getting, so just keep a strong sense of your surroundings. I tend to focus 25 percent of my energy on my feet, 25 percent on what the athlete is doing, and the remaining 50 percent on the shot I'm getting.

Second, be fluid. The followcam goal is to provide a compelling and interesting angle of the athlete, not to draw attention to you as the cameraman. This means that there is no better capture of a trick than the smooth, floating shot that you hardly notice happening. If you have trouble holding the camera steady as you go, think of every joint on your body as a shock absorber. Starting with your knees and hips, stay bent, loose, and be fluid. I keep my arm half bent so that even my elbow can absorb most of the bumps. If you ever get to see a Steadicam in action, imagine yourself as one when you operate: floating smoothly as the ground changes beneath you.

If you have a tendency to get low blood sugar and have trouble holding your hand out and still, then remember to eat before you go shooting. I always bring a Snickers or protein bar with me in case I get hungry. There's nothing more frustrating than trying to shoot with an unsteady hand.

The third and final key to a successful followcam shot is to know your athlete and what he or she plans to do. Followcam shots work best at close distance, in part because the long lens adds too much shake to move fast with it, and in part because the nature of the shot is to show movement — and nothing looks faster than when it's moving by up close. So if you're following an athlete, make sure you know their line

it's crucial to keep enough distance from the riders to always have an out. If they fall to their left or if their board goes right, be ready to move. On ramp, it's a whole other ball game.

If you've ever ridden ramps with more than one person, you know that your options are pretty limited as to where you can go. The whole back-and-forth part will keep the two of you in rather close proximity for the duration of the run. When you followcam ramp skating, you can no longer think of it as followcam; it's basically a doubles run. However, the key to shooting a single trick versus an entire run is very different. For one trick, you can drop in behind an athlete. As long as you know which way he or she will be turning, you can go to the opposite side and simply get out or sit down as the athlete does the trick. Basic moving-camera shots from the deck of the ramp and the bottom are also great angles to get while maintaining a certain amount of safety.

Figure 6-7 Shooting Shaun White from the deck of a ramp.

When it comes time to shoot an entire run, I approach it as follows: first, I think about how well I know the athlete and their bag of tricks. Many athletes are predictable in what they do, so by watching them ride as you shoot, you can tell what they're setting up for, and subsequently where they're going to go. In addition, if you know the person, it's always easier to ask about getting in the ramp with him or her for a run, which naturally can make any athlete nervous. My next step is usually to ask them what they plan to do before they drop in. Although many athletes will not plan every run, if you're filming in the ramp with them, chances are they'll make an exception. I often break down the tricks into three basic categories, each with its own three basic options. Table 6-1 lists some sample tricks and the categories into which they fall.

These categories allow me to simplify a run in my head and to more easily remember the line. Because most athletes vary a little on tricks from run to run, there's no need to plan out how high or far they will go — not to mention that you'll be able to judge distance based on their speed after coming out of the last trick. Next, if their run seems complicated, intense, or simply contains an element you're unsure of, ask the athlete if he or she can run it once without you. That way, you can see it play out, and plan your followcam line. As the athlete drops in for the practice run, imagine every step of where you'll be for each move. From wall to wall, it's important to plan what you will do. If they plan

Three basic options	Three basic categories		
	Air	**Grind**	**Setup**
Carving left	Alley-oop backside	Frontside grind	Basic air
Carving right	540 spin	Backside grind	Basic grind
Going straight up and down	Set-up air	Basic stall	Basic air & grind

Table 6-1 Sample tricks and the important element for planning followcam

on going for some risky or huge tricks in their "live" run, then, for the practice run, they can always just do basic moves as long as the general motion is the same (such as a carving air in place of carving 540). The final steps are to make sure you remember every aspect of the line before dropping in — and to make sure you have an out. It's very normal and likely with some athletes that they will mess up the line when the camera starts rolling, so don't just keep the shooting plan in your head — keep alternate plans and exit routes running too.

You can shoot followcam with anything from a cell phone to a 35mm film camera. But the easiest is always a camera with a handle on top. You'll also want to shoot with a wide-angle or fish-eye lens, and keep the LCD screen shut most of the time, going by feel almost entirely. This can take a serious amount of practice, but the result can be some of the most dynamic and compelling footage you'll ever see in a ramp. Try shooting a basic line without watching the LCD; as you do it, focus on what portion of the body you are aiming the camera at. Now watch the footage back and see if you were pointing too far up, down, right or left. If you thought that you were aiming at the waist, but you wound up shooting all head and no feet, then try it again — only this time, aim at their knees. Shoot, review, and retry until you find the right formula for you and your camera . . . then remember it.

Most three-chip DV and high-definition-video (HDV) cameras are the perfect size for followcam. The real challenge comes when you start using film cameras or ENG (electronic news gathering)–sized cameras. These weigh enough so that the agile movements that are often needed are now more difficult. These cameras are able to shoot followcam, but they add a layer of complexity.

When action-sports videos — particularly skateboarding, BMX, and in-line skating — became a guiding light of what was cool in their respective sports, corporate entities such as ESPN, NBC, and OLN (now known as Versus) began to catch on that followcam was a prominent part of the lifestyle. Even though, in the past, all X Games and Gravity Games events had been shot with ENG-styled operators, these companies now began to ask themselves the same question we all ask ourselves eventually: How can I increase the quality and production value of my

Figure 6-8 *Shooting by feel at the Vans Downtown Showdown. Courtesy Windowseat Pictures.*

shoot? In their case, the answer was simple: bring in the standard followcam skate video shots for the street and park course events.

In 2002, for the first time in history, followcam was brought in to the events. In the past, the concern had been staying clear of the athletes during competition runs and making sure all sports and riders were okay with it. It's one thing to be followed through a skate park by a friend; it's another to have someone behind you during a potential gold medal run. Thankfully, most athletes are now accustomed to followcam, and virtually none opted out during their prelims or even during the finals.

There is one more grand challenge that you may encounter if you plan to shoot multiple sports. Although almost all pro athletes get along exceptionally well, there used to be a real stigma between sports at an amateur level. This posed an issue for ESPN, and even for some riders who were concerned with their image. For me, I have been skateboarding since I was 12, but there is no better way to safely shoot a pro on a fast park course than with in-line skates. Just like shooting Rick Thorne on the streets of LA, the ability to follow even Freestyle BMX athletes over ramps and through a fast course is amazing on skates; no other device can get those kinds of consistent park and ramp shots. Eventually, ESPN gave skateboarding a more street-oriented course, so I began shooting followcam on a skateboard. However, if you're shooting at your local park and you plan to capture some scenes while you're using another sports device, I recommend feeling out the riders first to make sure they're okay with it. Get static shots first as they get comfortable with you and the shoot, then break out the board or skates when you know they're cool with it.

Figure 6-9 Followcam during competition runs. Courtesy ASA Entertainment.

Camera Settings, Lighting, and Filters

From followcam to other on-the-move shooting styles, there are a few key elements to making sure you're always getting the shot. The first is a basic trick every cameraman should know: the Z-scan. With action sports moving so fast on the ground, and the cameramen who shoot them keeping up while also maintaining equipment and a wealth of camera settings, it's all too easy to bump a button, flip a switch, or roll a dial while you're going. So here is a great way to avoid getting your shot, only to realize that your white balance got flipped.

Almost all of the information on your LCD and viewfinder is in the top or bottom row of the screen. This means that you can make a single fast scan of the information on a regular basis, in the shape of the letter Z, starting top left and moving across, then cutting down and over to the lower left, and continuing across the bottom left to right. This is a common trick used by the pros to make sure that they are regularly scanning their settings. Once you establish it as a standard, Z-scanning will become a routine pattern of your shooting that will help guarantee that nothing is off. The most common mistake can come from shooting a mixture of settings (for example, 24p and 30p) throughout the day. It's almost impossible to tell the difference visually as you're shooting, so this becomes an ideal place for Z-scanning to prevent mistakes.

There are wide ranges of tricks you can do to achieve certain looks within the camera as well. From filters to lighting, you can make your shots appear brighter, warmer, colder — even softer. The one thing you cannot easily change in post, however, is the lighting. So remember that what you get on the day for lighting may very well be what you have to stick with.

If you plan to light a scene, such as a single trick or just an interview, the most common and basic lighting setup is the three-point technique. For this, you set up a primary light, called a key light, to one side of the camera and subject so that it lights this side well, while casting only a small shadow on the opposite side. The second light is called a fill light. This light sits on the opposite side, and is used to fill in any

Figure 6-11 *Single onboard light kept below subject's eye line. Photo by Dave Mead, Windowseat Pictures.*

most flattering lighting you can do. A simple way around this is to either shoot them from below eye level so that the light is also pointing upward, or remove your light and have someone hold it, slightly off to one side and down. It may not sound like much, but in the right circumstance, the difference can be significant.

Finally, you may want to consider bringing a professional with you for full lighting setups. Called a gaffer, this person is well versed in all types of lighting equipment, arrangements, and even power requirements. A worst-case scenario might be your arriving on scene, lighting, bringing in your subject, then getting ready to roll — just as a fuse blows because too many lights were plugged into the same outlet.

Basic filters can thread onto the front element of your lens and create everything from colored effects to having no noticeable lighting effect at all. Although it technically isn't even a filter, many people like to use a clear, or UV, filter as an added level of protection for their lens. If you're shooting with the camera's standard lens, and not a wide-angle lens or a fish-eye, then a UV or clear piece of glass can help to guard against incoming skateboards or flying debris from a dirt bike.

Polarizers are one of the least expensive yet most helpful lenses to carry with you when shooting exterior daylight shots. They rotate 360

Table 6-2 *Popular filters and their primary uses*

ND (neutral density)	Used to decrease the overall amount of light entering the lens.
UV (ultraviolet)	Filter out UV light from the sun, or simply a great lens-protection filter to avoid scratches and dings.
Polarizer	Used to darken overly bright skies.
Colored filters	Used to make stylized shots or provide color-temperature changes to create warmer or colder shots.
Diffusion	Also used to soften harsh lights, these filters can provide a soft or dreamy feeling to the shot.
Cross	Used to radiate any light source into a star pattern. Most ENG cameras have this built in.

degrees, cutting out a portion of light (polarized light) that is entering your lens. By rotating the glass, you will be able to see the change in the cloud-on-sky contrast of a polarized image versus one that is not polarized. If, for example, you're shooting a lock-off of an athlete doing a trick outdoors beneath a very bright sky, this lens can be really helpful in balancing out the brightness.

Figure 6-12 *The effects of a circular polarizer. Courtesy Piccolo Namek, Wikimedia Commons.*

123

Figure 6-13 Action shot with a polarizing filter. Courtesy ASA Entertainment.

There is an ongoing argument regarding colored filters and diffusion for digital cameras in that most NLE (nonlinear editing) systems will now allow you to do a healthy amount of color correction in post. Final Cut Pro HD does pretty serious color correction now, therefore negating the necessity of these types of filters during the shoot. Many cinematographers will argue that the look of what you capture with filters during a shoot is in fact unique and cannot be replicated in post, but for most action-sports shooters, the time and cost of these filters isn't worth it in the field.

If you do want to play around, though, here's a cheap way to experiment. Diffusion filters can provide a very cool, dreamy, or ethereal look to the shot. Try taking a clear filter that you don't mind risking, and smear some petroleum jelly around the outer edges of it. If you do so smoothly, you'll end up with a very soft focus ring around your shot. Next, try smearing a very thin layer of the jelly over the entire filter. You've basically created a diffusion filter. This look can be great for dream sequences or artistic shots. Just keep in mind that as with all filters, once you shoot it, there's no going back in post to what the unfiltered image really looked like.

I remember speaking with Oscar-winning cinematographer Dean Semler for a documentary project, and he said that when he was shooting *The Alamo* with Billy Bob Thornton, they had huge scoping land shots that required lighting. There wasn't any easy way to hide the lights, nor was there a way to light the landscape from outside their massive wide shots. So the filmmakers would occasionally just leave the lights in the shot, knowing that digital technologies would allow them to remove the lights later (called painting them out).

The lesson learned here is that in post, with enough time or money, you can almost always make a shot look the way you want it. So sometimes you are better off not altering your shots too much in camera.

The only built-in filter included with most DV and HDV cameras is the neutral-density (ND) filter This is the most important one for your camera because it will allow you to cut out large amounts of light entering the lens, and therefore adjust your iris and shutter-speed settings to your creative preference. ND filters are essentially gray filters that can cut down or cut out light of every wavelength and color. One great use of the ND filter can be to lower your shutter speed below 24, so that it is open for longer than necessary, creating a unique ghosting or blurring effect. With the shutter open for so long, you'll be letting in too much light, so now kick on a single or double ND filter to compensate for it to find that perfect exposure (even close down the iris if necessary).

The resulting shot can be manipulated in several ways. For example, you can followcam a subject through the city at night and create very artistic, stylized motion-blur shots. Not only will the athlete begin to blur, but all of the passing cars and city lights will stream away from you. Another great shot is to slow the shutter a lot, and then lock off the camera on a tripod so that it has absolutely no movement. With a wide locked-off frame and a slow shutter, everything static, including the ramp or rail and surrounding environment, will appear crystal clear, while your subject grinds, slides, or flies through the frame in a moderate to extreme blur (depending upon your settings). Pretty much anytime you use a very slow shutter and lock off your camera, you'll get an interesting mixture of blurred and sharp elements. Figure 6-14 shows a shot I took coming into Los Angeles at night from a 737. The wing of the plane was static beause I had locked off the camera.

Figure 6-14 *Slow shutter of Los Angeles city lights from a 737.*

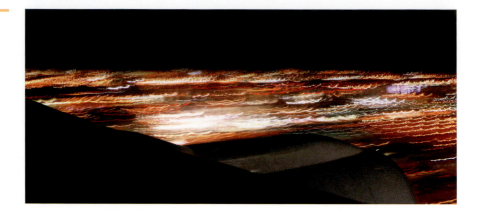

White Balance

White balance is a key factor in shooting all video. This is defined as setting what the camera sees as true white. Because every type of light has a different color temperature, always measured in Kelvin (K), it is important to set the camera to the appropriate color temperature (called white-balancing the camera). This will make sure that what you're shooting comes off with appropriate color or skin tone. Color temperatures can range from as low as 1800 K to as high as 16000 K (see Table 6-3). The high end of this range is far outside of normal use because even daylight peaks at around 6000 K.

Most prosumer cameras will come with standard white-balance presets and allow for at least one customizable setting. There are two principle types of light you'll need to understand: tungsten and daylight. The first

Table 6-3 *Primary color temperatures*

Kelvin	Common source
1700	Match flame
1850	Candlelight
3200	Tungsten lamps (camera preset)
4800	Sunlight alone (direct at noon)
5600	Daylight (camera preset)
6500	RGB monitor
9300	Television screen

is typically used indoors in standard home and office lighting fixtures, as well as in most skate parks. The second type is the color temperature of actual daylight. Both settings are usually presets on your camera, and are often referred to as Indoor versus Outdoor, or 3200 versus 5600.

A problem may arise if you choose to shoot in a mixed-lighting environment, such as a skate park with 3200 K tungsten lights as well as windows letting in 5600 K daylight. Depending on which light source is brighter, you'll have to either choose a preset or take a custom reading to find a balance. If you choose a preset — which I don't recommend — you'll end up with either a very cold blue light spilling in from outdoors or a very warm, almost red light coming from the inside. I usually opt for the blue spill because the opposite can result in skin tones appearing lobster red . . . never a good idea.

The second option is the custom preset. To do this, you'll first need to make sure that your camera has this feature; then you'll need to find a place at your location that has an appropriate balance of light from both sources. In mixed light, hold up an all-white piece of paper (or even a white T-shirt), and make sure that you are seeing only white through the lens, nothing else. Hit the white-balance button and wait a moment for the camera to read the light and process it. Once finished and set, the paper should appear closer to true white, and the environment and human skin tones will look better as well. This can be tricky, however, if the spill is not even throughout the room, so a few tries in various areas will sometimes be necessary.

You may also use your white balance in place of filters. If you're shooting outdoor action sports on a cool, overcast day, but you want the image to look warm and sunny, try this little trick. Take off the preset 5600 Daylight setting and go custom. Next, find a light blue surface such as a T-shirt or wall that you can frame up and use to white-balance the camera. Using this surface to white-balance is essentially telling the camera that what it sees is supposed to be pure white. To compensate for the blue hue, the camera will automatically add orange, or "warmth," to the picture. The result will be a much warmer-looking frame for you to shoot in, which will in turn help to create the feeling of a sunny day. Just don't shoot the sky!

Figure 6-15 *3200 K tungsten/indoor white balance with blue daylight spill.*

Figure 6-16 *An overcast cool day with warming filters. Photo by Dave Mead.*

Basic Tricks and Unique Angles

Okay, so you understand most of your camera settings and options. Now it's time to play with various angles. Because most action-sports videos are either documentaries or music-driven montage projects, there are very few issues with continuity and camera-placement rules. Even so, it is important to understand a few of these basic rules when shooting. Let me start out by saying that all rules in film and video production are simply guidelines. No matter who you are or what you're shooting, remember that these rules were established because they work 99 out of 100 times — but for that one time that they don't work, the rules must be disregarded. Filmmaking on any level is a creative endeavor, and your vision is the only thing you must be true to, not the "rules" of filmmaking.

Having said that, the first basic precept is the 180-degree rule. This is an imaginary line that is established with your first shot in any scene in which one or more subjects are positioned in any one direction. The idea is that if you cross the line in your next shot — say, to the other side of your subjects — there will be a continuity break because your subjects will now be looking or facing in the opposite direction. If you are shooting more than one athlete talking, perhaps a guy and a girl, and the guy is on the left in every shot, then, when you jump the line, the guy will appear to be on the right, and thus looking in the wrong direction. This can be jarring or confusing to your audience.

In skating, if an athlete grinds a handrail right to left in a wide shot, and then you cover it in a close-up but from the other side, the athlete will suddenly appear to be going left to right. In montages, this can be a technique to create an intense feeling. The confusing or jarring emotion that a viewer will get from jumping the 180 line can be a useful tool if the mood calls for it. It's a serious attention grabber, which might be the goal for a montage of an incredible trick.

Another basic rule is to always make sure you cover scenes and shots from various distances, focal lengths, and positions that are all different enough from each other that it won't be too jarring. Say, for example, that you shoot a trick straight on and then decide to shoot another take

129

Illustration 6-1 An example of the 180-degree line and where your camera can go.

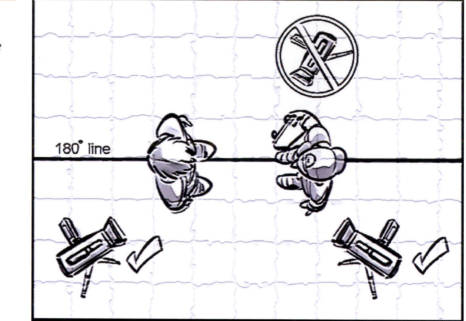

of that trick. You plan to cut to the second take from the first take, but you move only slightly left or right of the original shot (less than 30 degrees). The result is that you'll wind up with a jump cut between the two shots (more on editing in Chapter 9, Postproduction).

A favorite angle of mine is the Dutch angle. This is basically done with the camera canted slightly to one side, creating an off-axis shot. The Dutch angle originated in the 1930s in German films. The German word *Deutsch* actually means "German," and was adapted to today's "Dutch" when referring to that style of shot. It can make for a very interesting angle for establishing shots and any frame that contains a great deal of straight lines in it, such as the sides of buildings. I would recommend, however, that you avoid Dutch angles of grinds, airs, and any trick in which you are panning or tilting with the athlete. The reason here is critical to understand, and is based largely on what you are shooting. Many ENG-style operators shoot Dutch angles of action sports as a means to add excitement to the scene. This is naturally ingrained in their shooting style because regular news shots can often use a little spice (consider a flat, static shot of a street sign versus starting off Dutch, then whip-panning to the sign). Dutch shots can be great

Illustration 6-2 *Avoid a jump cut by placing the camera at least 30 degrees away.*

if it's a news piece for the media or other mainstream audience that might appreciate the added camera "spice" more than the trick itself, but most action-sports videos avoid the Dutch shot because it can be such a distraction from the trick itself. Let's say Bob Burnquist is doing a McTwist (an inverted 540 on a ramp), and as you pan with him up the ramp, you decide to Dutch the camera while he spins. There's a good chance it'll either look like he's spinning off axis, or perhaps not even going inverted at all. Most enthusiasts therefore prefer to see the trick clearly on video, and enjoy it for what it is alone. So if you're making a core action-sports video, use Dutch angles only when the shot is a wide lock-off or for artistic shots — but rarely during close-up or medium panning and tilting shots.

If you've ever shot a vert ramp from the side or bottom, you'll notice that sometimes the tops of the walls do not appear to actually reach a vertical point. They may appear angled, or just under vert, based on the angle you're shooting from. One trick you can use to help excite your shot slightly is to Dutch down a little opposite the wall of the ramp, helping to bring it back to vertical. Because you're looking up at an off

Figure 6-17 *A Dutch lock-off shot of a handrail. Courtesy ASA Entertainment.*

angle anyway, the Dutch in this case will be hardly noticeable or distracting. Instead, it'll help to make the stunt look as difficult as it truly is. While we're here, I think it's also critical to mention the importance of these low-angle shots. All too often, we see huge stunts in the media or action-sports tricks on TV that are shot from sweeping overhead angles. However, low angles make tricks and stunts look bigger. Just like the classic Hollywood hero shot of Will Smith or any other actor rising to vanquish the villain, when you get your camera down low, and shoot up at your subject, you'll create an empowering and even heroic feel. This feel will translate into tricks of all sizes, making them appear bigger and more impressive. If you're shooting an FMX (Freestyle Motocross) rider clearing a 100-foot gap, try getting low near the center of the jump, maybe even far from it, and just making that jump look as enormous as it actually is.

If you're going for straightforward standard action-sports video, and you've seen your share of videos, then of course you can always imitate and do what's come before you. However, I'd encourage you to push the limits of what's out there. Consider what might be new and different, and yet still cool. It's key in all progressive industries to do just that: progress. And all too often, the sports progress without the video creators who capture the athletes themselves progressing. There is something to be said for the fish-eye lens, a standard shot that captures most of the latest stunts. However, it's the rare video that pushes that boundary with clever camera use (such as the Girl/Chocolate *Yeah Right!* video) and becomes a standout among the rest. Maybe you wind up shooting some old-school Super8 film of tricks, or perhaps you plan to link together every shot in the video with camera movement. Whatever your idea, just have one, and stick to it. Video makers will try to tell you what's the right way and what's the wrong way to shoot an action-sports video. At the end of the day, remember that the only rule — the only thing that you need to be true to — is your vision.

Documentary vs. Reality

Controversial documentary filmmaker Michael Moore refers to his work as "nonfictional personal essays," which raises a very real question as to what is and what isn't a documentary. Merriam-Webster defines documentaries as "of, relating to, or employing documentation in litera-ture or art,"[1] — and then goes on to reference words such as "factual" and "objective." So if you're out capturing professional or amateur skaters in their natural environment, then it's safe to say you fit the definition.

Unfortunately, television isn't always so clear. The newest genre we've all grown to love and hate is reality TV, and this is the closest thing to the documentary format that television has. From shows such as *Viva La Bam*, starring pro skateboarder and troublemaker Bam Margera, to *Rob & Big*, featuring pro street skater Rob Dyrdek, these programs blur the lines of reality. Many top-running reality shows are extremely out-lined, produced, or — worse yet — even scripted. In a way, reality has become just another fictional genre used for entertainment and viewer escapism. The irony here is that escapism used to be about those big over-the-top action films in which John Rambo would rescue POWs from Afghanistan. The problem is that that's pretty much what people see on CNN nowadays. Escapism is now reality, and reality is now

---

[1] *Merriam-Webster Online Dictionary* (www.m-w.com).

escapism. So the idea of capturing real life, the more dramatic the better, has literally upped the ante of what is entertaining.

In many ways, this benefits action-sports filmmakers because the nature of what they're shooting is intense. Consider several of the record-breaking reality shows of the beginning of the 21st century: *Survivor, American Idol,* and even *The Amazing Race.* All of these shows put people in a situation in which a lot is at stake — and typically, to the viewers, the more at stake, the better. It's like all the old action films where one person must save the world. The difference now is that it's not total fiction, and there actually is something at stake. Although what's at stake is not saving the world, it can be completely intense because it's real. This is why you have a unique opportunity to make something that pushes the limits of entertainment. Action sports have a built-in reality aspect because so much is at stake every time a skater drops in, a skydiver leaps off, or a snowboarder charges a kicker.

Figure 7-1 *Launching out at Pipeline, Maui. Photo by Dave Mead, Windowseat Pictures.*

Arnold Schwarzenegger appeared in the 1987 film *The Running Man,* in which he fled for his life on a fictional reality-TV show. What made the film's story ahead of its time is the likelihood that this may be where entertainment is actually going. Danny Way jumped the Great Wall of

China, Travis Pastrana pulled a double backflip on a dirt bike — and what will happen next, no one knows. Action sports are progressive, and you have a unique opportunity to tell a captivating story. Just remember: media is an ever-evolving entity itself, and what is popular this year may not be next year.

Moving Forward

So Michael Moore makes personal statements, or "essays," in the form of what once was the documentary, and of course reality TV and web shows are not actual reality. These are facts. If anything, these shows and movies should encourage you to think outside the box, look at what's new in the world of media, and consider where things are going.

When you set out to make a documentary, you may have a basic idea of what you hope to get and how you'll cut it together. There is no solid line as to what exactly is and isn't a documentary. The idea that you are capturing real people doing real things is enough for most viewers. However, if you want to script your project — perhaps to make a commercial, perhaps a short series of webisodes or clips for the Internet — then you'll need to decide early on.

Figure 7-2 *Frame grab from the scripted "Danny Way Skater" clip, as seen on YouTube.*

Scripted shoots require much more organization and planning than documentaries do. You will have to decide well in advance who will be in what scenes and how you want those scenes to look and feel. The biggest difference between scripted shoots and documentaries is that scripted shoots often require more time, more crew, and more equipment. A typical documentary crew can be as small as you alone, to the more typical one cameraman, one sound person, and one producer (see Figure 7-2). This three-person documentary crew is all it takes to make a high-production-value project. So long as your camera and sound people are experienced, you can make a theatrical-ready project with this simple setup. Just keep in mind that the basic action-sports video is typically shot alone on a single camera.

Scripted shoots can also be done with few people involved; however, they usually do take more time and more personnel to do them right.

Figure 7-3 *A standard three-person documentary crew. Photo by J. M. Kenny.*

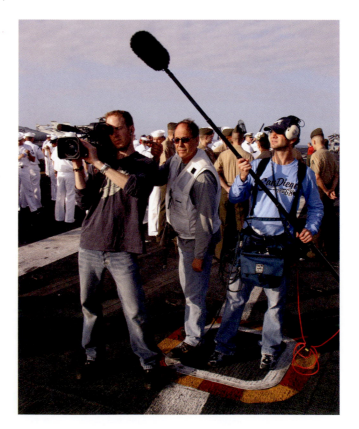

Of late, many action-sports videos have begun to intercut scripted elements (or story vignettes) within the action. From high-profile selections such as Birdhouse's *The End* to under-the-radar small productions, you can find a decent selection of mixed-format videos out there. This growing format of mixing documentary and scripted shoots together is likely to stick around for quite a while as its popularity with most enthusiasts of action-sports video continues to grow. A main reason for this is the use of nonactors in the scripted clips. Although most athletes have had their share of time in front of a camera, most of them are not trained or experienced actors, which can add an element of entertainment or flat-out fun for the viewer. Getting to see an athlete you follow and enjoy featured in a video skit usually goes over quite well.

Getting the Interview

Many of these mixed-media-format projects also include typical action and interview fare. There are three basic types of interviews we are going to discuss: the OTF (on-the-fly) interview, the sound bite, and the sit-down interview.

OTF interviews are like sound bites. They happen on the go, in the moment, and usually with little or no planning. A good OTF can take place in the middle of a crowded room, on top of a ramp right before a contest, or even while skiing or snowboarding down the side of a mountain. The beauty here is that most OTFs capture the athlete in their natural environment. They allow for your shots to further the story of who this person is. A Summer X Games athlete putting on his pads as he gets interviewed is the perfect example of an OTF. It's also nice that the OTF allows you to get both present tense and past. There has always been something so powerful about interviewees talking about what just happened when they are still standing in the moment at an event. This sense of urgency plays very well in both directions, past or present. If you ask an athlete what just happened or to describe what a friend did, you are basically getting an intro for the trick itself — a compartmentalized little story, if you will. On the other hand, if something is happening in the background as the interviewee is speaking, he or she can essentially be calling the shots in real time, giving you present-tense sound bites.

Which leads us to the next style of interview, the sound bite. This can be a very gray area as to when it stops being a sound bite and when it starts to become an OTF. In short, the sound bite is essentially an excerpt from a longer speech or a quick man-on-the-street comment. Although a sound bite can be as short as a few words, it can also run as long as several paragraphs. What makes it a sound bite is that it stands alone as a single item cut into something larger (more on this in Chapter 9, Postproduction). Some of the best sound bites happen with absolutely no setup or planning at all. Whether I've been on the deck of a ramp, by the ocean on the beach, or at the base of a ski resort, I can't count how many times I've been rolling and just happened to get a random comment from someone close by.

Figure 7-4 Dave Paine shooting OTFs with BMX legend Mat Hoffman. Courtesy ASA Entertainment.

When you interview an athlete, there are a multitude of questions you can ask. Some of the more typical ones asked at action-sports events are shown in Table 7-1. I always find that bringing a list of possible questions with me on a shoot or to an event can be a great help. If you haven't done many interviews before, then make a list and review it before you go in for an interview. There's nothing worse than finally getting that perfect moment with a top athlete and running out of things to ask!

Another helpful tip that always sounds overly simple is this: as you're talking to an athlete, remember to pay close attention to his or her answer. It's very easy to focus too hard on what you want to ask next, and thus lose focus on what your interviewee is saying. You'll find that a balance of each (what he or she is saying, and what you want to ask next) is necessary for a great interview. Consider what your next question will be as they're speaking, while also thinking about what they're saying and how to transition out of it. If you ask them about what they plan to do in their next run, and they begin talking about some pretty crazy tricks they are planning, then perhaps ask them next about the difficulty of those tricks or the fear involved. The key to a great interview is to listen and keep it flowing. Most

Table 7-1 *Popular questions asked at action-sports events*

- Start with simple questions such as name, age, hometown.
- Have them explain what's going on or where they are.
- Ask them why their sport's important to them, why they do it.
- Have them pick a rider they like, and talk about that person.
- Ask them what makes great style.
- Find out which competitor they think will win, and why.
- Have them talk about how events compare to riding with friends.
- Ask them about the most impressive thing they've seen today (or be specific — you should know which shots are your strongest).

athletes will give you more than enough time if they feel you aren't wasting their time. Too much inappropriately timed silence or thinking on your part can send an athlete rolling away and end an interview early.

The final interview style is the sit-down interview; it's the most thorough question-and-answer session you can set up. It usually requires a prearranged, more formal interview plan and a quiet location. Most sit-down interviews take place away from the noise of a major event because they tend to dig more deeply, with personal questions that may not relate to a specific event. A good rule of thumb is that the only time background noise should be heard is, first, if you can see it, then second, if it relates specifically to what is being discussed. For example, if an athlete is talking about his or her life as a skater in the city, and in the background you can see and hear traffic, then it'll feel natural to the viewer. If you shoot them by a playground, however, and the sound of children yelling is audible but you can't see them, it'll likely be just a distraction. You'll also have trouble editing the interview because the background noise may be inconsistent throughout it.

Figure 7-5 Vans Cup Tahoe interview couch on the mountain. Courtesy Windowseat Pictures.

Interview Locations

Location is everything for interviews, from sound quality to distractions to what the background will look like. One of the most intriguing and unique interview setups I've ever seen was done for the Rail Jam at the Vans Cup Tahoe in 2006 and 2007 (see Figure 7-5). Director Bill Kiely worked with action sports DP (director of photography) Brooks Ferrell to create the very natural feeling of the interview set on the hillside right next to the competition. This is a perfect example of putting your subjects right into the action you might be hearing, while keeping the environment appropriate to the content.

It's always best to find a location that fits the vibe of the athlete or conversation. Many action-sports production companies will try to lock down a location for all their interviews, then run power out to it, set up lights, and bring athletes over to the area one at a time. The quality of a well-lit, patient interview will show, so if that's your goal, then spend your time on it.

Although it will vary in importance to every interview, lighting is usually a key factor. Most interviews on location are shot OTF style, with no lights. On occasion, a single light (such as a sun gun), a bounce board, or diffusion for the bright sun will be used, but typically it is more raw and in the moment. Even night shoots often rely on existing lighting or a single onboard light for the camera. But sit-down interviews are different. Cameramen/DPs will usually try and take their time setting up lights and making the set look and feel comfortable. For this reason, interviews are often shot indoors or, at the very least, in the shade; the sun can be a very harsh source of light (for more on lighting, see Chapter 6, Shooting Techniques).

Don't Be Afraid to Ask for What You Want

I spent a great deal of time early on in my career giving the interviewee too much power. When I would do question-and-answer sessions, I would be afraid to push where the interview was going, or I would be afraid to lead the questions in a direction that better fit my story. The truth is that when you're interviewing, you have a choice: be a producer or be a director. Although some people argue there is no director in documentary filmmaking, it's a much grayer area than that. Consider again Michael Moore, perhaps the greatest example of a man who directs his pieces with an admirable precision. His work may cover popular topics in reality, but they do so from a stance he believes in. Many argue that an opinionated stance is antithetical to the documentary process.

Figure 7-6 *Snowboard filmmaker Chris Edmonds capturing life on the mountain. Courtesy Tim Peare.*

Many filmmakers (that is, directors) don't like to be called producers, even on documentaries where they are putting much personal style into the pieces and are hardly just producing them. This battle exists on projects of every size.

So how can you tell if you're directing or if you're producing? The answer can be as simple as your personal choice or as complex as dissecting how much and to what extent you are shaping the piece. If you lead the interviews, craft your story, isolate characters, and progress your story visually through your shots, then you are directing. If you simply show up, ask a provided list of questions, and hire someone to capture what is happening, then you are producing.

When it comes time to go after your interview with a strong goal and purpose, as a director would, you will need to think of your talent almost the way you would think of actors. The catch is that you can't speak to an athlete interviewee the way you would an actor, so you must be clever and considerate. As you bring up topics you want to dive into, and as they begin to answer, you should identify the key elements of the answers that best fit your story, then ask them to go deeper in that direction. If you are creating a specific vibe or tone in your piece, then help bring them into that tone by setting the tone yourself. If you are rushing and speaking quickly, to keep an urgent feel to your piece, they'll likely follow suit.

When I was shooting interviews for *Harnessing Speed,* I wanted several of my key interviewees to get their tone and attitude back to how it had been months ago for the subject they were discussing. So off camera, before I started asking questions, I had them go back to that day and talk a little about what had happened. This allowed them to freely revisit the emotions that they had felt early on, and then maintain that tone and feeling during the actual interview.

Now granted, there's a fine line between guiding the interviewee and putting words into their mouth. It's a line that you have to ride delicately and cautiously if you want your piece to be a real documentary. Most of my early interviews were simple; they incorporated the types of basic questions listed in Table 7-1. But as time progressed, I came to realize that the truly compelling interview actually requires you to get into someone's head and help bring out of them the details and emotion that you won't get when you stick to the surface questions.

Another interesting technique is to consider what tense they will be answering in. Most sit-down interviews happen after the fact, and are more or less recaps of an event from the past. This can give the viewer a more distant feeling of the event — a feeling that can work both for and against you. In some cases, you will want to try to re-create the power of what actually happened in the past. For this, I will sometimes have an interviewee outline what happened off camera, then, on camera, take me play by play through that event as if it were happening right then. For example, if an athlete landed an incredible trick for the first time, and you have ample B roll of that day to cut away to, then shoot for sound bites. Here's an example: "I'm staring at the rail and thinking, 'I can do this,' but I know if anything goes wrong, especially with that drop on the other side, I could really hurt myself." This technique can be very powerful for putting your viewer right there in the moment. It does, of course, require that you have enough footage of the subject to cut away to for most of the interview — such as shots of them looking at the rail, preparing to try it, noticing the big drop, and then going for it.

Figure 7-7 *Pro-athlete interviews.*

Every interviewer faces a delicate balance of pushing and getting compelling material without offending your subject. Especially in action sports, it's critical that you maintain a friendly, easygoing relationship with the athletes you shoot. If you don't know them personally, then go easy in the first interview (or at least the first interview questions), and feel out how far you can push things before you risk ruining the interview or the connection. Most athletes are used to interviews and the basic questions that most interviewers ask. They may not be used to more-meaningful or more-intense questions, so it can be helpful to prep them before the interview with what direction you plan to go in, to make sure they're okay with that. Nobody likes to be blindsided on camera.

Although sound bites and OTF interviews will be the more common flavor you'll encounter, I encourage you to push the boundaries of what's normal and accepted. Be it for skate videos, documentaries, commercials, reality shows, or webisodes for the Internet, in the ever-changing medium of film and digital content, there is no right and wrong way to do it.

As noted, the complexity of your story can vary greatly. You don't have to be making a narrative piece to still consider how to best tell your story. Like the illustration above, it can be as simple as an athlete trying to land a new trick or even covering in detail a trick itself. One of the most popular analyses of dramatic structure is built on five acts and came from the famous 19th-century German writer Gustav Freytag (see Illustration 8-2).

Illustration 8-2 The German Gustav Freytag's five-act dramatic structure.

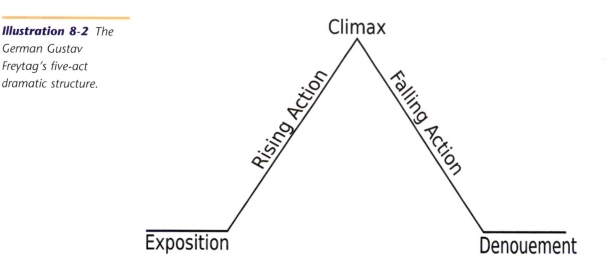

In its simplest form, the foundation for a character arc or story is best described by the Greek philosopher Aristotle in three basic steps: a beginning, a middle, and an end. Consider the story of Tony Hawk's landing the 900; it was powerful and emotional. Tony's story was that of the underdog: a man struggling to overcome the impossible. Act 1: Tony decides to try a trick many had thought impossible. Act 2: Tony's repeated attempts and failures begin to stack up as the fans cheer on. Finally, Act 3: Tony lands the trick, and victory is his. This story was iconic for action sports, demonstrating to the mainstream audience just how amazing the stories in these sports and their athletes can be (something many athletes already knew from their own personal failures and victories).

If you aren't shooting Tony Hawk, or even an impossible trick, then consider the simplest forms of story you can still tell, such as your friends going to a skate park for the day. Act 1: several friends leave the house and head to the skate park; they arrive, check out the surroundings, decide what to do, and get ready to roll. Act 2: the session of tricks, falls, and interaction between the friends; some of them land new tricks or pull off old ones on new obstacles; others get hurt and decide to throw in the towel. Act 3: some with victory and others with defeat, they all leave, and the day ends (see Figure 8-1).

This may seem like a very basic way of breaking it down, and it is, but this three-act summary shows just how simple storytelling can be. A random montage of back-to-back tricks — with no sense of who, why, where, or when — will almost always leave viewers confused or just not as fulfilled as they could have been. The only exception might be when you're making a trick video solely for fans of those riders, and all the fans care about is seeing the latest tricks. Even here, though, some sense of who, what, and why will help.

Although you may get away with minimal stories, you should always have structure. It'll give your audience a sense of geography, and this can make all the difference between whether or not they enjoy your project.

Figure 8-1 *Act 1: A group of friends take a road trip. Photo by Chris Mitchell.*

Figure 8-2 *Act 2: A session takes place at a skate park. Courtesy Windowseat Pictures.*

Figure 8-3 *Act 3: Heading home for the day.*

You should try and always incorporate the basic key elements of storytelling, which are plot progression and character arcs. If you are documenting real athletes, then character arcs will be mostly out of your control, but like the triumphant arc of Tony Hawk, it is critical that you keep your eyes open for them as they begin to form. When you shoot any road trip, documentary, or other project in which you're following a group of people for any length of time, you should quickly try to identify which ones are the most outgoing, colorful, and open to the camera — these athletes could make great main characters and possible storytellers themselves. Then decide who is the most likely to overcome or accomplish something great throughout the shoot — this might be your character arc. By identifying these personality types early on and quietly watching them develop, you will get more material and better material because of your knowledge. I always try to have a few key athletes I use regularly for updates and info on camera. They're the go-to people for when something happens and I need a quick sound bite of what went down. If you don't identify people early on, you run the risk of grabbing anyone in the moment and either being rejected or simply not getting a good sound bite.

The Dangers of Working Too Close

Coverage, coverage, coverage. If you haven't got that in your head already, it's a crucial element for you to remember. The more you can shoot on the day, the more options you're going to have in post, so always shoot for coverage. Even a snowboarder hitting a jump is a mini-story in and of itself. Even Aristotle would likely break it down to the takeoff, the air, and then the landing as your three-act structure. Because of this, it's always crucial to get in there and get the coverage. Unique angles and creative shooting may put you right in the middle of the action. Although this is great for creativity and storytelling, it can also get dangerous.

From annoying athletes by being too close to their tricks, to focusing too hard on the shot when a board comes flying at your head, there are

Figure 8-4 Capturing athletes at the LG Action Sports Championships. Photo by Mike Opalek.

many critical reasons to keep your eyes open when you're getting in close. Minor risks can be worth it because the up-close-and-personal coverage will also give your viewer a more intimate feeling of what and whom you're shooting. Fish-eye lens shots of grinds and general sound bites up close with athletes are always great things; the more you cover, the more likely you'll have enough material to make a successful piece.

At those times when you have to be so close that you're in harm's way, you have a few options for getting the storytelling shots without getting wrecked. Keep an active stance, not sitting down or hanging over an edge. If you keep one leg far enough behind you, you'll be able to pull out and get away quickly if the athlete loses control.

These up-close-and-personal shots can cut perfectly with long-lens distant shots on the same rail, ramp, or obstacle. When you arrive for the session with friends or to shoot pros at an event, take it all in before you start shooting. I prefer to stay wide and consider all the angles I

Figure 8-5 *Keeping an active stance. Courtesy ASA Entertainment.*

might want before I gear up. You'll also have a chance to capture some of those storytelling moments of interaction between friends right before a session begins. These personal moments can add a lot to a section when athletes are considering what they might do or talking about what they're afraid of. Once they start warming up, you can use this opportunity to back off, give them some distance, and get your wide masters. As the athletes begin to start hitting tricks, this is a great time to now start working your way in for the coverage. Eventually, you should try to get in tight and grab some close-ups, but keep a strong sense of awareness of how welcome you are. If an athlete is getting annoyed at a trick or frustrated with anything at all, he or she might redirect that anger at you if you're too close at the wrong moment. Essentially, you just want to keep one eye on your shots (developing story), and another on the riders and their attitudes.

"Make It Sexy, Jazzy" — and Why Someone Said That

It was 1998, and some friends and I were doing stunts for a TV movie. Several skaters and industry people were involved in the film. Beyond that, it was a fairly studio (or corporate, as the description goes) production. The director of the film was very laid back, a nice guy with a great knowledge of directing. His understanding of action sports, however, was limited.

On one particular day, take after take, we would charge down a hill, hit a ramp, and fly into a series of large PORTaPITss landing pads. It got to a point where the director wasn't happy with how it looked, and we were going as fast and as far as was possible, so he began to get frustrated. The technical adviser on the project was Chris Mitchell, a former athlete and X Games writer and photographer with a great sense of composition. Chris asked the director what was wrong, and he responded that "it doesn't feel right," followed by a frustrated: "Make it sexy; make it jazzy." Essentially, what was happening was that the camera placement was too high for the tricks being done; it didn't show the intensity or complexity of what was happening, only the story element. Chris helped find an angle that best captured the action of the tricks — and all of sudden, the shot worked.

The point of this story is that what the director was seeking is the same thing we all look for in our shots: compelling angles that are either unique or tell the story best. His terminology may have been foreign to most action-sports enthusiasts, but his intentions were the same.

Building Suspense and Drama

Aristotle wrote many great bodies of text, including *Poetics*. Though most of it was lost through time, *Poetics* explains the importance of suspense for building and creating drama. Aristotle wrote of how critical it is to have elements of impending danger, yet to maintain some degree of hope. In many ways, this is the very principle upon which action

156

sports are built. Every trick, every progression within every sport, is done out of hope that it is possible, though the clear and present danger is always there.

World champion in-line vert skater Eito Yasutoko, and many before him, knew just how to build up this suspense for an audience. In many ways, Eito is a pioneer of action sports; he has pushed the limits of what is physically possible on a half-pipe. At contests, his fans expect Eito to do new tricks with more rotations, higher out of the ramp. And it is at these events that he has mastered the art of building suspense for a live audience. Whether it's a Best Trick contest or a demo for fans of the sport, if Eito comes out with an enormous spin or flip trick and falls repeatedly before landing it, the emotional response from the crowd is far more powerful than it would have been had he just pulled it off first try. This is a very basic show technique that crosses over to film and video as well.

You may not be able to shape when an athlete lands a trick, but if there is a serious degree of difficulty involved, then shoot enough coverage and get enough sound bites to properly build up the suspense in the edit. Again, coverage, coverage, coverage. On the other hand, if you have scripted a project and the athletes are working with and for you, then help create the suspense within your piece by establishing the danger and risks early on. Clearly show how wrong things could go, and add in a countdown or a ticking clock of some sort.

In 2002, I was shooting a documentary on the making of *xXx* with Vin Diesel *(xXx: A Filmmaker's Diary)*. The first week of shooting was called the drug farm; it was the film's opening segment, featuring an exciting escape on a dirt bike. The sequence included numerous FMX jumps over exploding elements while military helicopters were firing weapons at Vin's character, Xander Cage. The culmination of the scene was that the entire large barn in the center of the field would explode while Xander was jumping it. To help create the suspense for this section, we took cameras inside the barn during prep and showed just how many explosives there were. For safety's sake, the prep time was long, which meant the night shoot was racing to happen before the sun rose. So we built up the element of a ticking clock by constantly showing the fight to beat the sunrise. Then, through the use of suspenseful music and intercutting sound bites with the cast and crew, the countdown to the stunt began. With the audience well aware of just how dangerous this stunt actually was, there was no lack of suspense in the final edit. The film cameras begin to roll, and the explosives all go hot. Xander pins the throttle and hits the jump; he goes airborne as a helicopter rises behind him, firing round after round. The special-effects team triggers the explosion, which engulfs the barn and the air around it in a massive fireball — and Xander, staying true to that splinter of hope, flies clear of the fireball and lands, riding to safety away from the flying debris.

The three-act structure, the ticking clock, the looming sense of danger — all of these things helped to tell the compelling story of what happened that day. Even if you're not shooting explosions and large movie sets, these tools for building suspense will still apply. The ticking clock can be established in any environment at almost any time. You can show it visually between an athlete and a big trick they're about to do by intercutting the approaching danger, alluding to what is basically a countdown to when the "event" is going to happen. The key is to identify how you can best implement these elements based on what you have to work with, and then move forward. If you are making a docu-

Figure 8-7 *Rob Cohen, director of xXx, on set. Courtesy Sony Pictures.*

mentary, just be patient and pay close attention because some of the best story arcs will come together while you're shooting.

Documenting a Road Trip

One of the most common formats in action-sports video is the road trip. If you plan to hit the road with a group of athletes, there are some very key elements you will want to cover. First, you need to identify what your story is. It might be a group of friends going away for a weekend to ride, or it could be about an epic spot you've heard about, and you're all going out to find it. There's no limit to what story you can tell, but defining one will help you know what the goal and tone of your piece will be from the beginning.

The next key element is preparation. Make sure you have everything you need to properly cover the trip. From camera gear and batteries to weather gear and flashlights, pack the necessities. It's no big deal if you overpack, but remember: there's no home or office to duck into if you forget a charger or other important gear.

Figure 8-8 *A simple night shot with an onboard light. Courtesy Todd Seligman.*

Assuming that the basics of the trip are already taken care of (food, transportation, places to stay, and so on), now it's time to start shooting. It is a good idea to do a brief sit-down interview or some OTFs (on-the-fly interviews) with your athletes prior to the trip. Ask about expectations, who's going, where they're going, and why each one decided to do it. Your questions here are part of the first act of your journey. This is where you want to set up some goals that you hope to achieve, as well as to establish that sense of geography for your viewers. The scope of the trip should also come across in pretrip interviews.

Now it's time to hit the road. To tell a road-trip story completely, it's great to get a few shots of the departure. If you can get an exterior of the car pulling away, without your getting left behind, go for it. This shot could be picked up (or cheated) at a later time if the location you're departing from is fairly generic looking. The real goal here is to get the emotion — the excitement or nervousness or impatience of the "here we go" moment. This might be a great place for a montage later in which you can add voice-over, so get plenty of B-roll shots on the road. Table 8-1 has a list of some key B-roll shots for road trips and montages.

As you get into the journey and begin to document everyone on the trip, you're going to want to start to build characters. If you are going to get your audience involved in your athletes — whether it is to love them, cheer for them, or even not like them — it is key that your viewers have a sense of who these athletes are. To do this, you want to focus on capturing the unique traits and quirks of each one. Examples might include showing that someone is always asleep or being messed with by the others, or perhaps one of them is always on their cell phone or smoking, or maybe there's a funny one in the group. Just as in documentaries, these characteristics are important parts for road trips because

---

Table 8-1 *Classic road-trip montage shots*

- Speedometer at speed
- Yellow dashes on the road going by
- Key highway signs such as location and towns
- Interesting roadside billboards and signs (capture local flavor)
- Establishing shots of your athletes in their vehicles
- Character-building shots of the athletes
- People sleeping, eating, laughing, staring out the window
- Landscapes and the passing world
- Road-trip vehicle in motion (tires spinning, passing by places)
- Sunsets and sunrises

you're relying on people's interest in your characters as much as their interest in the tricks. Don't be afraid to capture too much of these character-building moments; just keep a respectful eye on how receptive everyone is to your filming.

The next key element in a road-trip documentary is arrival at the location. As you begin to get close to the area, you should be ready to roll the camera and jump out and stay with everyone if they stop and get out right away. Although it is good to try to get establishing shots of where you're pulling into from inside the vehicle, remember that you can always go back to get those later. You can't reshoot an athlete's reactions to when he or she first sees the location, so concentrate on those shots when you arrive. Cover the reactions of the athletes while they look out the windows in excitement and anticipation. When you come to a stop, you can either follow them out, or even ask them to let you out first and give you 30 seconds to set up so you can shoot their exit. This latter option is a question of how much you want to cover and how willing they are to work with you. If they aren't willing to hold up life for the camera, then go with the flow and get what you can. As the athletes exit, there's nothing wrong with cutting from inside the vehicle straight to one of them hitting an obstacle if it suits your story.

Figure 8-9 *A snow-boarder about to begin his session. Courtesy Windowseat Pictures.*

The primary goal of shooting a road trip is still very similar to how you'd shoot most action sports locally; the real difference is that you'll want to include more lifestyle and personality shots than you normally would. Capture athletes reacting to each other, interacting with each other, and doing any of their unique character-building traits you centered on earlier. The real goal here will be to get enough footage to cut together a solid riding section. Whereas most trick videos are all about the latest and best tricks, sessions in road trips are more about the people and the story of the trip; so here, you can get away with shooting more-basic tricks because your audience will be engaged with the story and the characters, and not just waiting for shots of the next trick.

Finally, as the day finishes up and you either head home or move on to the next spot, you should capture closing sound bites or OTFs of the athletes recapping how it all went. You won't want to show much of the return trip home unless something monumental happens, but you should shoot it regardless to try and get any shots that you missed on the way out. Getting a few shots of athletes sleeping, resting, and being worn out from the trip can always be a nice close to your story. You can also think of the return trip home as a take two of the entire trip out. Because the athletes may be bruised and tired, this is a good opportunity to get all of your cutaways of the passing world.

When you get back home, it's a good idea to set up interviews again with the key riders you've shot the most (or even all of the athletes). Talk about how the trip went, if expectations were met, and what the vibe was like coming home. As described in Chapter 7, you can even have them recap some of the days in present tense so that you can intercut B roll of the actual day over the interview.

In the end, if all goes well, you will have a complete story that takes viewers on the road, introduces them to some interesting characters, and gives them closure to the events of the road trip. The format of the action-sports road trip has been used in everything from typical skate and action-sports videos to true-to-form documentaries. Perhaps most legendary in this format is the original 1966 surf film *The Endless Summer,* in which director/cinematographer Bruce Brown followed two young surfers around the world, trying to find the perfect wave. This film is a prime example of just how much heart and soul a road-trip story can have.

Figure 8-10 *A setting sun ends the day. Photo by Dave Mead, Windowseat Pictures.*

Trick Tips and How-tos

A final popular action-sports segment you might want to make is the how-to section. Sometimes referred to as a trixionary (trick tips), this section usually features a single athlete talking into the lens, explaining how a specific trick is accomplished. Because this format usually takes place in the moment, it's okay to not shoot formal sit-down interviews, and instead focus on OTF-styled sound bites at the location of the actual trick.

Whether it's how to land a snowboarding jump or how to drop in on a mini-ramp on a bike, trick tips have become very popular online and in the media. After creating an athlete-participant wiki site devoted entirely to defining and explaining all tricks in action sports (wikitrick. com), I was shocked to learn how many participants are eager to find out how tricks are done. The ease of creating how-to segments has made them very popular. With the progressive nature of action sports adding new tricks every day, it's no wonder people want to learn and see how new moves are accomplished.

The format of the trick tip is simple. It usually opens with an athlete introducing himself or herself and explaining the trick they're going to break down. That's typically followed by footage of them setting up for the trick, or even seeing simpler versions of the trick, which act as stepping-stones. This all typically culminates in multiple angles and even slow-motion playback of their trick. If the athlete discusses an intricate detail of how to grab the board or lock onto a rail, then you might want to cover that element separately from an angle that best shows the detail.

Because the goal of trick tips is essentially to share the knowledge of how something is done, the most important thing is usually the information, then, second to that, the artistic shooting style. You can get very creative in how you cover the athlete and trick. Just remember that the ultimate goal of the piece is to clearly explain and show a trick.

Postproduction

The final step in the process of film and video production is "post." Postproduction will include all aspects of the post process as listed in Table 9-1. This step can literally shape your piece in any number of directions. Even with the narrative story you've shot, you'll have options from sound to colors that can change the entire tone and feel of your project.

Table 9-1 *Important stages of postproduction*

- Tape logging and organization
- Capturing or digitizing footage
- Creating an assemble edit
- Editing rough cuts
- Adding a sound track
- Adding sound effects
- Locking picture
- Adding special effects and CG
- Locking the audio (sound design, VO, music, etc.)
- Color timing
- Mixing
- Rendering
- Outputting

Film editing took place originally on machines or by hand. Many college film schools offer classes that begin with splicing and viewing film on a Moviola or a flatbed such as a Steenbeck (see Figure 9-1). This is where you can learn to appreciate the finer details of film and the editing process. It is, however, not as efficient or easy as today's technologies. As discussed in earlier chapters, nonlinear-editing (NLE) systems have taken over (see Figure 9-2).

When I was in college, the first editing course I took presented an experiment in which they gave everyone the raw, unedited film (the dailies) from an episode of an old television program called *Dallas*. We were not given a script or any guide as to what the writers or director had intended, but we were asked to review the footage on our own and then edit the show however we thought it best played. As you can imagine, the result was a massive variation in versions from student to student. People put scenes in a different order; shots were cut side by side in one show, then nowhere near each other in another. The pro-

Figure 9-1 *Steenbeck film editing by hand.*

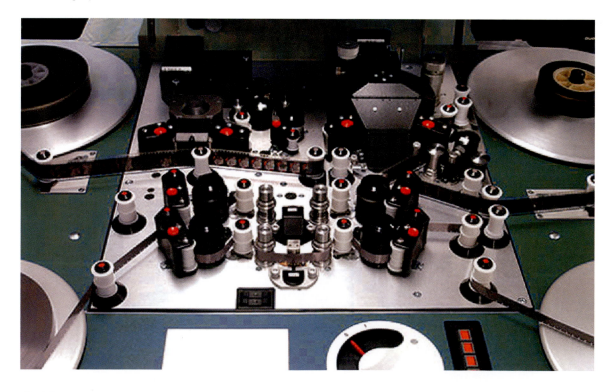

Figure 9-2 *Nonlinear/ digital editing. Courtesy Apple.*

fessor's point was made. It was simple: no matter what you shoot, no matter what you intend to make, it all comes together in post. There were no wrong answers. Every edit that I saw worked and was entertaining. As you sit down to cut your project, consider that regardless of what your original intention was, this is now a new step with a virtually clean slate.

Many directors and producers of action-sports videos will stay heavily involved, if not do it themselves, throughout the post process. I find that, if possible, it can be a great help to have someone else involved. Chris McKinley, a very talented editor whom I met in college, has cut a good many projects with me over the years. Although I might have final say on what I'm going for in the end, I will always ask Chris to make his first cut on our projects without my being involved. This is usually called an editor's cut or rough cut. There have been countless times that Chris will think that a shot I'm in love with is completely useless to the story, and I'll realize he's right. Or he'll look at shots and make connections between them that I never saw. Giving someone whose opinion you trust the freedom to make a clean pass on the project can open your eyes to ideas you may never have realized. If you must cut alone, then I strongly suggest getting a friend to view the edits as you go. Your friend can offer constructive criticism as to what feels right and what doesn't. You don't want to believe that the piece is done, and screen it for a group of friends — only to conclude that the pacing is off or the shots all linger too long. Don't be afraid of feedback; it's always an ally.

Logging and Selecting

The first official thing you should do when you wrap a shoot is consider backing up all your tapes. Digital video (DV), high-definition video (HDV), and other small-tape formats are not nearly as stable as large formats such as HDCAM and Digibeta. Most tapes will last many years, but these smaller formats are more susceptible to scratches and tears that can result in digital hiss or other glitches.

It's crucial to also label all of your tapes exceptionally well. I'd suggest tape numbers for capturing, then also include dates, locations, and any key elements you may want to revisit down the road. Five or ten tapes may not seem like much, but after years of shooting, you can end up with hundreds or thousands of tapes. A simple mistake early on, such as writing the day and month but not the year, can haunt you later when you're trying to find a shot from your early days of shooting. To many people, old footage is just that: old. So why keep it around or organized for later? The answer is that ten years from now, you may shoot a new video or spot with an athlete, at which time you want to show how far they've progressed or what they looked like when they were young. I've even had companies approach me for stock footage or repurposing my tapes as cell-phone content and web videos based on old segments I shot with pros.

Once you've labeled, you're going to want to decide if you need to capture all your footage, or capture only selects (the shots you think you'll use). Prices for hard-drive storage drop every year and will con-

Figure 9-3 *Keep your tapes organized and labeled.*

tinue to do so, which can mean hundreds of hours of DV or HDV storage on a small external drive. It will be up to your system and your budget to decide if you have the space. I have always edited DV and HDV on a Final Cut Pro HD system using a Mac Pro desktop with ample internal SATA drives striped together (see Figure 9-4), as well as a few external FireWire 800 drives. For high-bit-rate HD footage, you'll need a much faster system (see Chapter 2, The Tools of Action-Sports Filmmaking). The upside to capturing all your footage is the time you'll save by letting tapes digitize unsupervised, and not worrying three weeks from now about looking for that one shot you didn't capture. Some editors like to make notes and watch the footage capture, but I feel that if you shot it and know what's there, you can spend your time more wisely scanning through it after the footage has been captured at a faster rate. In any case, you should do what works best for you.

One more key consideration in capturing is what codec you will capture in and through what cables. Digital cables such as FireWire and USB 2.0 connect directly to most computers and cameras, and carry a signal that includes tape timecode. If you accidentally lose your media later, you'll be able to batch-capture any one of your tapes by opening

171

Figure 9-4 *Mac Pro with four internal SATA drives. Courtesy Apple.*

up the autosave backup versions of your project. To do this successfully, you are going to need to clearly label all your tapes, and make sure the label information corresponds exactly to what you enter when you begin capturing each tape.

DV, DVCAM, HDV, and a few other formats will allow you to use FireWire cables to capture. Most higher-end formats will have too much information associated with the footage to travel through FireWire. As a result, you can sometimes capture FireWire for your off-line (lower-res) edit for these higher-res formats, but to get the full quality of what you shot, you'll need to later use an online HD edit bay to batch-capture. The problem most people see in DV codec is that it compresses the footage quite a bit to get so much into such a little space. Although you may have shot DV, that doesn't mean you need to edit in it. Every time you capture, record, lay back, output, or re-anything in the DV codec, you are compressing it again. Most projects won't show a difference with a few compressions, so if you shot DV, then you may not be worried about getting the pristine image that true HD offers you. But if you are concerned, you can consider capturing in a higher-quality format such as uncompressed 8 bit. This will help maintain the quality of the footage you shot, but it will also take up a lot more hard-drive space. I usually keep DV projects in DV, then output them in uncompressed 8 bit for DVD burning or tape mastering. If the DV footage is part of an HD project, then I capture and work with it in uncompressed 8 bit before finally up-resing it to HD.

Editing

If you have a script, then that's the ideal place to begin by assembling and laying your shots out in order. On the other hand, if you were shooting a road-trip or trick-montage project with no script, then you're going to want to sit down with all of the footage and begin a paper edit. A paper edit can be as simple as a basic outline with approximate running times, based on how much usable footage you think you have for each section. It can also be as detailed as laying out your shot order, song choices, and even selecting interview bites.

One creative decision that differs by person is whether you begin to rough out your project with or without music. Some editors love to choose a temp or final track of music to cut to; it's a great way to set the tone or pace of a scene. Other editors will first lay out everything in a single broad stroke, then slowly make sweeping passes over it, adding layers of revision and polish as they go. Either way, editing is an art form. In many ways, it takes trial and error to discover a process that will work best for you.

As you begin to find a structure that works well for you, you'll need to consider at what point in your edit a sound track and sound design will be temped in. If you have someone composing music for you, then it may be best to be editing to a track as close as possible to what the

Figure 9-5 *A Bucky Lasek trixionary editing timeline.*

final will be. You can also hire a sound designer, responsible for adding sound effects and various supporting audio work such as Foley.[1] Sometimes sound effects can make such a significant difference in how a piece feels that I'll even begin to temp them in early on in the process to get a better feel. These effects can come from stock sound-effects libraries, which you can find online, or even from creative programs such as Apple's Soundtrack Pro.

If you shot a documentary or trick video and you don't want to do a paper edit, then your options are twofold. First, you can cut to the music. This is a popular technique in action-sports videos because their lack of a unifying story will leave the footage without a sense of structure. By using music to create structure, you're giving the viewer that important sense of geography. All music has a definitive beginning,

---

[1] A Foley artist in a film is a person who records and lays down environment and general sounds such as footsteps, doors closing, and so on.

middle, and end, so if you incorporate 10 songs for a 35-minute video, then viewers can skip to their favorite section throughout the piece.

Editing to the music often involves cutting shots to and off the beats. Many skate videos will go so far as to make sure that every trick is further emphasized by having the rider either take off or land right on key beats of the music. Rarely are videos edited with the shots themselves cutting on the beats. This is because the tricks are far more important than the editing in most montages and trick videos. Don't let that fact discourage your efforts as an editor, however; remember that almost all editors possess the incredible power to make a piece have far more impact than it ever could have if it had merely been slapped together.

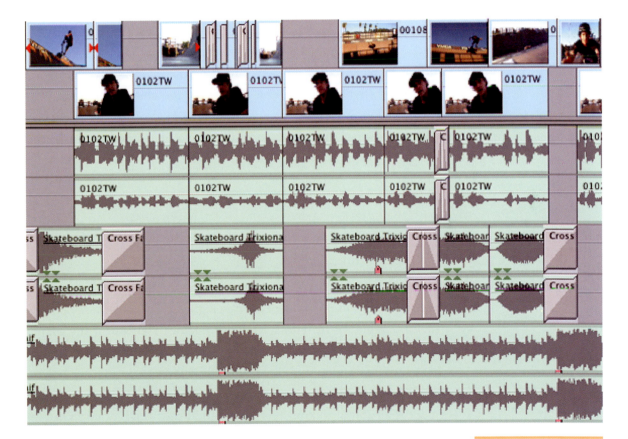

Another great perk of cutting to the music is that you have the innate ability to create rhythm visually. Many times the pacing of a piece will feel off if longer shots are intercut randomly with shorter ones, and vice

Figure 9-6 *Cutting to music-track beats as seen as a waveform.*

versa. With music, particularly with good music, the pacing has already been set in a way that is pleasing and smooth. Even if you are cutting dialogue or a scripted piece, many editors choose to use music as a guide for beats and rhythm.

The second option you have is to add a score (original music) to the edits. This is the classical way of editing, in which you will cut the entire piece or section first, based on how you feel it should go, then lay the music down second. In the event of sound tracks, this is a far more difficult way to go because the song in the sound track is already locked in pacing and tone. However, if you are composing your own tracks, then you will be able to match the music almost exactly to the visuals.

This technique requires a bit of planning ahead so that music can be smoothly put to the order and pacing of the visuals. If you don't consider the timing of your edits before trying to compose music for them, then you or your composer may find it hard to constantly change up the tempo or rhythm throughout the piece. Film editors often cut with beats and tempo in mind, depending on the goal or feel of the piece. An action sequence might be accelerating toward a climactic finish, and so the edits will be getting shorter and shorter as the pace of the piece speeds up. As this is happening, the music is also accelerating to match it all. The result of a seamless visual and audio scene of this nature will be a suspenseful, edge-of-your-seat experience as that big finale approaches.

Many action-sports videos will have elements of the climactic ending, depending on the flavor of the project. The climactic finish in Jamie Mosberg's Birdhouse film *The End* (see Figure 9-7) is a perfect example of this technique. In the end scene with Bucky Lasek and Tony Hawk skating and playing against each other, the pace rapidly accelerates to a massive visual and audio climax in which Bucky triggers explosives, killing Tony and becoming the number one skater. The pacing of this segment is all edited to a powerful Propellerheads track titled "On Her Majesty's Secret Service," which grows electronically and in orchestral intensity to enormous proportions and, eventually, a big finale.

But perhaps you aren't going for that suspenseful climax or ramping "pedal to the metal" pace. Maybe you're just cutting a chill surf video

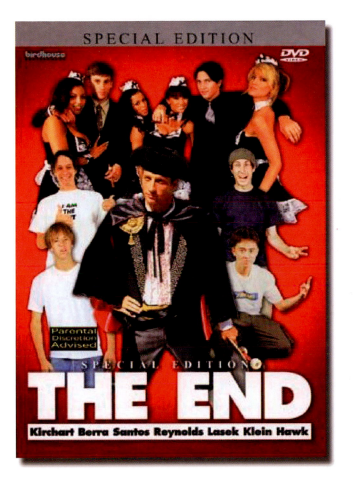

Figure 9-7 *Climactic finale from the Birdhouse video* The End.

or slow-motion lifestyle piece. In those instances, you're probably looking for a much more relaxed pace and editing style. This can be achieved through the use of dissolves, longer shots, and fewer cuts per minute. Whereas the fast-cut, upbeat pace of a video can have as short as three- or even two-second shots (that's nearly 30 cuts per minute), the video with a more relaxed pace can average five- to ten-second shots (or even longer, for that matter). Many artistic shots can be slowed down in post, taking the pacing of your video to a whole different realm of visual candy. An amazing trick in your sport, or even an amazing shot, can often warrant a post slow-motion effect. Although some cameras can shoot slow motion in camera (see Table 9-2), most cannot. Chances are, you will need to slow down the footage in the edit bay. Final Cut Pro

177

Table 9-2 *Some cameras that shoot variable speed*

- The RED ONE digital camera
- Sony HDW-F900H
- Sony PDW-F350 XDCAM
- Panasonic AG-HVX200
- Panasonic AJ-HDC27H VariCam

HD, for example, will offer seriously slow speeds, but you'll be degrading the quality of the footage for every bit that you slow it down.

Standard NTSC video shoots at approximately 30 frames per second.[2] Assuming you want to run the footage at 50 percent speed but didn't shoot that speed, then you'll need 60fps to do it. In order to calculate and render that shot at 50 percent, edit programs will go through a complicated process called interpolation in order to add frames between the ones you shot. If you do this effect in post, though, and then scroll through the new shot frame by frame, you'll see that every other frame or two has a ghosting image that may stutter on your screen. This is the result of the interpolation because those added frames were technically fabricated. The only way to bypass this and get true crystal-clear slow motion is to overcrank[3] while shooting film and video.

It can take some toying around in post, but by experimenting with slow motion at slightly different speeds (say, 40 percent versus 60 percent), and depending on what shutter speed and frame rate you shot your video at, you can find an ideal slow-motion speed for your footage.

---

[2] 30 frames rounded up from NTSC actual 29.97fps, as discussed in Chapter 2.

[3] Overcranking, or shooting in slow motion, is a reference to when film cameras were hand-cranked. So by cranking faster, you were shooting more frames per second than was needed. This meant that in regular-speed playback, the image would be in slow motion.

Editing Film

If you shot film on your project, then you're most likely going to be cutting that film digitally. In what is quickly becoming the old days, film editors were called negative cutters. They would actually splice an entire movie or documentary together by hand. With growing postproduction technology, now most film shoots remain only as film, until the developing process.

Exposed film is taken to a developer, where reels are spliced together, processed (or developed), then sent on to telecine.[4] The resulting footage can be of any quality, ranging from low-quality videotape (for screening purposes or off-line rough cutting), all the way up to 4K digital files that are of movie theater quality. If you've opted to shoot film and go through this process, then you're most likely going to be finishing the post process with your tapes, and not the film, from this point forward.

Top action-sports videos often incorporate 16mm and Super 16mm film, so this is a common process for many film and video producers. If you take this route, the telecine house will also give you a disk with Flex files on it, along with your tapes. If you plan to ever go back to the film for any reason, then these Flex files will be important in the post process. If you don't need to go back at all, then you should be okay now to move forward without them. Flex files are a series of codes that will help to translate, frame by frame, your video timecode to your film's Keykodes (the numbers running along the edge of the film). Many top programs such as Final Cut Pro HD come with software that integrates the program seamlessly for importing your Flex files for editing. The final step from here will be to batch-capture your footage into the computer. Now you're ready to cut!

If you're cutting on a nonlinear system, or even cutting film by hand, there is a strong difference between being an editor and knowing how

---

[4] Telecine is the now-common process of transferring film to a videotape or digital format. Telecine machines project light through the film as it runs, sending an image to a sensor for recording.

Don't worry; you're not going to jail over it all just yet. I know that rights can sound daunting at first, but consider this subject to be the fine print of the music industry. With the large volume of user-generated content and ease of file sharing on the Internet today, publishers are scrambling to hang on to any control they can with content they own. In the same fashion that you should be paid for your finished action-sports project, so should musicians get paid for the use of their music in your video. At least, that's how the industry feels.

There are countless online and other music clearance-professionals who can go through your list of music and, for a small fee, take care of all the paperwork, phone calls, and effort to grant you the rights, or clearances, you need to make a free-and-clear piece. There are also several options that don't fall explicitly under the four rights mentioned above. One of these options is if you choose to record a song yourself, or "cover" a band or track you like. In this case, you will still need to get certain rights for the copyright owner of the original piece of music, but you may not need all of the mechanical rights and master rights. Oftentimes this can make it a great deal cheaper when you're trying to get rights to popular tracks from the past.

The next exception to getting all the rights comes in the form of the two sweetest words in production: "public domain." The best definition I've ever heard for public domain says very simply that it's anything that can't be claimed as owned or private property under copyright law. Unfortunately, public domain can also be somewhat of a gray area.

Essentially, once a work enters public domain, it is no longer owned or protected under copyright law. The terms for public domain have changed over the years, so read up online or ask a lawyer to make sure you're clear about this. The oldest, most common standing law dates back to 1909, and says that 75 years after the last surviving author passes away, the work enters public domain. This means that any work falling into that category is fair game, and you can use it without getting a license.

One of the aforementioned gray areas, however, is if the work has been rerecorded by another artist, or if it first appeared within another work that is copyrighted by another party. For example, if you take the rock version of Beethoven's Fifth Symphony that was recorded in 1985 by Falco, it was certainly recorded long after Ludwig van Beethoven died in 1827. Although the original version of the music is fair game, this newer version is not, because you don't have the mechanical rights from Falco. As another example, let's say you use a version of Beethoven's Fifth that was recorded by an artist who died in 1925 and left no surviving owners. Because both the performer and composer are now public domain, and because more than 75 years have passed since their deaths, then you may use that version without obtaining rights.

A final important note on public domain is that the rules do not apply to every piece of material. On both sides of the fence, there are exceptions that can work either for you or against you, so check with an attorney before you do anything. There are even a few nice perks out there based on various slipups and accidents in the public domain. For example, some television shows, such as four Three Stooges episodes, have wound up in the public domain by accidentally not being renewed.

Figure 9-9 *Some* Three Stooges *episodes are even public domain.*

So you have the basic understanding of music rights, but now you want to know if you should even bother with them. That's the million-dollar question. There are two very distinct schools of thought on this. If you buy a CD, edit it into a sports video of you and your friends, then give out copies to your buddies, technically, you still need the rights to the music. However, if you contact a big publisher and try to get the rights for this scenario, most of the time they won't even want to deal with you on such a small project. Now any logical person might deduce that if they don't have the time to take what little money you have now (when you're offering), then odds are they aren't going to take the time to harass you later. I've seen this logic hold true for a great many projects that all operate "under the radar" of big publishers. Many times, if your project is distributing low numbers of units (by Hollywood standards) — such as a couple thousand, as compared with large projects that distribute tens of thousands or even millions of units — then you might find it difficult or even impossible to get all the rights to the music you want. Of course, it is always better to follow the letter of the law if you're unsure.

There have been instances when small projects have become popular and then turned big. In the case of a few select recent skateboard and snowboard films, video producers opted not to get rights to their projects in the beginning. Then, when their videos became hugely successful, they suddenly popped up on the radar of the music industry. The video companies then found themselves getting legal letters that often came in the form of a cease and desist. This essentially means that the company has to either immediately remove all product from the stores, swap out that record label's music, and reship every copy they have — or simply call the label, negotiate to purchase the music, and hope for the best. The problem here is that they're now negotiating for music clearances with a publishing label that isn't too happy with them, and on a project that has already proved successful. This is a lose-lose scenario. If you're making a film or video that is going to incorporate owned music, then do yourself a favor and speak with a music-clearance professional about how to proceed.

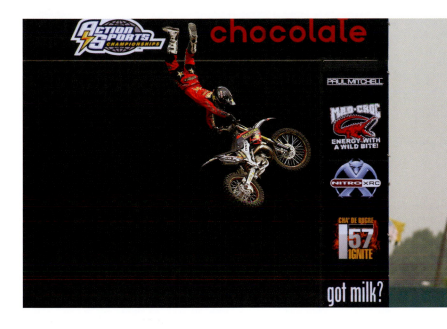

Figure 9-10 FMX at the LG Action Sports Championships.

Visual Effects: How, What, and When?

Visual effects have long been a tool that filmmakers have used to enhance or help tell a story. Only in recent years, with the proliferation of inexpensive effects programs and increased computer power, have pieces that are entirely effects driven become standard. From animated films to shots enhanced by visual effects, you'll see some level of visual effects in almost anything you watch today.

Visual effects can come in all shapes and sizes. Typical action-sports effects include computer-generated imagery (or CGI) that is often composited into live-action shots. This can come in the form of opening-title sequences, chapter cards created in Apple's Motion (see Figure 9-11), or even enhancement to shots themselves. In the case of Spike Jonze's *Yeah Right!* video, the visual-effects work in the more popular sections involved the removal of green skateboards to create the surreal illusion of athletes floating over handrails, streets, and curbs.

185

Figure 9-11 *Sample effects in a chapter card.*

Because visual effects involve the manipulation of frames of video, usually over long periods of content, the process can be slow and meticulous. Most complicated effects are done frame by frame, which can result in hours or even days of work for some shots. Computer processing power, which is responsible for the time necessary to render these shots into real time, has thankfully been growing exponentially over the years. This added power results in faster renders and better effects.

Top effects programs for working with video come in a wide range of prices and styles. The most popular program, and possibly the longest running, is Adobe's After Effects. Very similar to Photoshop, this program simply adds time to the dimension of work space, allowing users to create and alter images in almost any way, and then to duplicate and track those changes over the duration of the shot. Other popular programs include Apple's Shake and Motion. After Effects is a fully functioning visual-effects program that integrates almost seamlessly with Final Cut Pro HD, allowing for everything from stabilization of shaky footage and keying of blue and green screen shots to the creation and manipulation of advanced digital imagery. Motion, on the other hand, comes with Final Cut Pro HD Studio and has a very intuitive user interface that allows for advanced particle and text generation, motion-graphics creation, and much more.

All of these programs interact directly together, which can be a great asset when editing and doing the effects yourself. A final top effects program is Autodesk's Combustion, which does most of the same effects as listed above, and operates as a smaller version of the far more powerful Inferno and Flame compositing systems. These latter systems have a great history in Hollywood for top commercial and film-effects work throughout the years. Some people feel that they're overkill for small action-sports projects because most Apple programs are bundled together and less expensive, although it should be noted that some of the lower-priced programs aren't as capable as their higher-priced competition. If your work consists primarily of shooting, editing, and then doing effects on your own for smaller action-sports projects, then chances are you won't need the processing power or complexity of a high-end system.

The key to most visual-effects work is the idea that less is more. Visual effects should be nothing more than a tool you use to get your project to its destination. Much as you'd use a wide lens and long lens to shoot your piece, visual effects and CGI should support your project, not define it.

A cautionary tale can be taken from a recent experience a college friend of mine had with his first big project. Throughout college, he skated and made skate-related projects, always with a strong understanding of visual effects. This knowledge of effects helped to get him

Figure 9-13 *The cutting-room floor.*

aside. Thanks to today's digital technology, you can put unused shots in a bin and consider them later.

If you're an editor by nature and you know what feels right, you may still spend heaps of time trimming as opposed to cutting. Directors are notorious for trying to add or remove even single frames from a shot's head or tail. Any editor will tell you that a single frame really can make a difference. I've seen cuts of 45-minute action-sports documentaries that distributors or producers said felt "long." They then asked the editor to cut 5 or 10 minutes out of the piece. Now that may not seem like much when it's not your work, but cutting more than 10 percent of what was already the best of your best can be quite painful. The solution? Try going back in and trimming frames from almost every shot. Oftentimes the pacing of a piece is not directly related to how many shots it has in it, but rather, to how tightly packed together the shots are. Every time you introduce a new shot and the users have to refocus on all the new information, you're holding their attention. This technique is simple but very effective, and usually won't result in an edit that is that much shorter.

Let's say that you've now decided it's time to picture-lock your project. The effects, the cuts — everything in your timeline is locked. You're ready to output now, which means you'll need to decide what format. As mentioned earlier, any format can be digitized in any number of codecs. This means that you don't necessarily have to output in the same

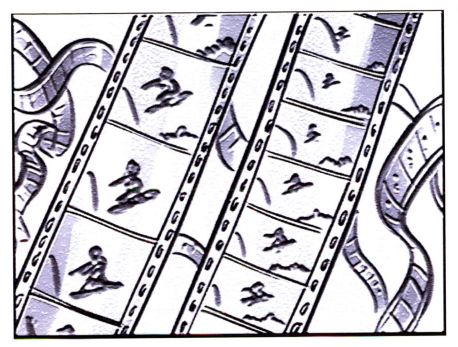

Illustration 9-2 *By tightening shots instead of cutting them, an edit can feel much shorter.*

format you captured in. If you plan to duplicate your project, you should talk to the dub house and ask them what format they prefer. They may not want a miniDV tape, or perhaps they don't have an HDV playback deck. Many duplicators will accept DV tape, but they'll prefer a more solid tape format such as DVCAM, BetaSP, or Digibeta. Newer dub houses will sometimes allow you to bring in uncompressed Quick-Time files on a data disk or external hard drive. This latter option will save you a single-generation loss and allow you to deliver the highest quality possible, even if you can't afford it.

When I shot the Bucky Lasek trixionary for the LG Action Sports Championships show on CBS, they asked that I deliver the final cut on HD. I had shot the piece in 1080i/24p at variable frame rates on the Panasonic AG-HVX200, and then edited it in Final Cut Pro HD on my own system. The problem was that there wasn't an HDCAM deck available, so I instead outputted from the editing program as an HD Quick-Time file, and then simply burned it to a disk. This allowed me to deliver pristine-looking HD content without needing a pricey deck or HD tape stock.

can, save and back up your project's EDL (edit decision list), then output another copy of the film with split audio tracks. Separate the music onto one track, and the rest of the sound (dialogue and sound effects) on another. This way, if you do need to swap out or pull a music track down the road, you can do so easily and quickly. Hard-drive prices have been dropping, so you may also want to back up any important projects for future use. I try not to dump media (delete it) from any project nowadays; if possible, I purchase a small external drive, and copy all projects, media, and related files onto it for safe-keeping. I have made videos that featured one athlete, and then, years later, we decided to do an expanded piece on that athlete. Having quick access to the original bin in which he or she had been placed became a real asset.

Finally, remember that if you are shooting to disk (such as the Panasonic AG-HVX200 with P2 Media cards), and not to tape, then you aren't going to have tape backups of your footage at all. In this case, hard-drive backups are critical. As a general rule, just keep all footage online until you absolutely have to dump it — and even then, stop and consider all of the possibilities for your project before you make a decision.

Distribution

10

There are millions of people on this planet with great ideas, but only a handful ever execute them. Distribution is the final step in a long process that many people don't ever finish. If you're ready to distribute your project, then whether you think it came out good or not good, you should be proud of yourself for having completed it.

A film or video can be distributed in many ways and many forms. In the past, studios controlled most theatrical-distribution outlets. At the same time, getting on television or into home-video stores was almost as difficult, if not impossible. Thankfully, it is far easier to get your material out there in the world we now live in. To help understand not just where your options are, but also where they are going to be in the coming years, here's a little history of distribution.

In 1938, the Supreme Court of the United States decided that film studios represented a monopoly. Imagine a world where only one studio's films could play in theater chains — chains owned by that one studio. Eventually, the ruling led to the independent distributors that operate today. In the past, these distributors would have considered only big-studio features and the occasional independent film that popped up on their radar. Today, however, there are countless new technology-driven distribution opportunities emerging each day. In addition, with an estimated 2007 U.S. box office revenue of $10.16 billion[1] and growing annually, never has the public been so financially and socially engaged in this industry.

Distribution companies can no longer afford the luxury of wearing horse blinders to the small projects being developed every day. From action-sports documentaries to independent films with action-sports themes, many of which are being shot on prosumer-level gear, the chance for your project to make it into theaters is more realistic than ever.

Illustration 10-1 The process from home video to theater has never been so easy.

Various online-distribution opportunities have changed the options you'll have. Large companies such as Netflix and Blockbuster have begun opening their doors to "cold call" submissions. If you're making a small project with little or no intent of distributing it, yet you'd still like to get your video out there, then your best option may be the

---

[1] Nielsen Entertainment/Nielsen NRG, MPA Worldwide Market Research & Analysis.

Internet. You can find countless avenues online for submission of your project and for having it be considered for full distribution.

In the past, top action-sports home-video distributors — for example, JustPushPlay — would review your film, get it into niche shops, and then consider pushing it to mainstream stores such as CompUSA and Best Buy. These companies are still top names in the industry for action-sports videos; however, your distribution options have now expanded.

Table 10-1 *Leading distribution outlets*

- Film festivals
- Home video
- Theatrical
- Television
- Internet

Film Festivals

In 2001, the Sundance Film Festival saw yet another unofficial spin-off of its titanic popularity with the action-sports festival: the aptly titled X-Dance. Taking place annually in Park City alongside Sundance, Slamdance, and a slew of others, X-Dance has gone on to become far more than just a Sundance spin-off; X-Dance quickly established itself as its own event, with quality submissions from throughout every division of the action-sports industry. The 2006 X-Dance Best Picture Award went to *Full Circle*, a top Freestyle Motocross documentary on X Games gold medalist Nate Adams. The documentary chronicled Nate's incredible rise and fall and return to the top podium. In 2005, the award went to Jack McCoy's *Blue Horizon*, an incredible surf film by Billabong that documented two very opposite surfers: two-time world champion Andy Irons and soul surfer Dave "Rasta" Rastovich.

As the leading action-sports festival, X-Dance has provided an outlet for many action-sports videos to shine. X-Dance has helped projects receive accolades that led to distribution deals and provided a screening ground for projects in need of a formal premiere. Like most film festivals, X-Dance is open to submissions from around the globe. If you've created a project and have little or no outlet for distribution, a great place to begin your research is with film festivals. You'll also find that by attending a festival, you can get a great understanding of what's out there and what's on the horizon.

Figure 10-1 *Park City, Utah, skyline at night, home to X-Dance Film Festival. Photo by Todd Seligman.*

Although not all projects are right for festivals, many festivals evolve in what they are looking for. There have been years when revolutionary trick videos have won at a festival, only to be followed the next year by a biographical documentary. If your project is right for festivals, a good starting point would be for you to research what projects have won at those festivals in the past. It should also be noted that many action-sports festivals are available online on a centralized web site called Withoutabox.com. This site offers the ability to create one user profile for your project, and then submit that same profile easily, and for a discounted rate, to countless film festivals. Because there are a growing number of festivals all over the world, this can save you a great deal of time, as opposed to going through submissions one at a time.

All film festivals will require a screener copy of your movie on or before their final deadline. Remember to check with them to make sure you have the dates; otherwise you risk waiting another year for that festival. Some festivals will have extended deadlines, and others will

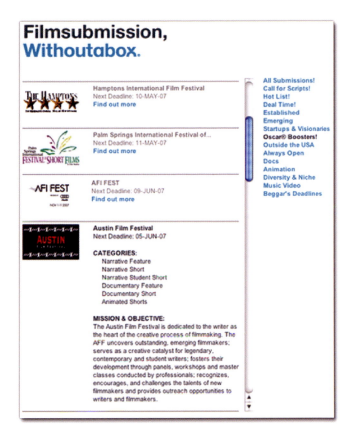

Figure 10-2
*Withoutabox.com offers
film-festival submissions.*

even allow rough cuts to make a deadline as long as you can guarantee you'll have your final cut ready in time if you get selected. You'll also need to put together some basic material for a press kit. This typically consists of a brief synopsis of what your film or video is about, bios on the filmmakers and any principal actors or athletes, and possibly some photographs that might spark the interest of screeners and viewers. If you're writing a bio and synopsis, try to make them stand out. Although festival screeners want truth and honesty, they do receive thousands of submissions, so a unique or memorable project may well get more attention than others, thus increasing your chances of getting in.

There are two schools of thought on film festivals. The first is that new, small festivals are unknown, and thus worthless to the serious filmmaker. This side of the fence believes that you should spend your time and money submitting only to notable and respected film festivals. The other side of the fence argues that, although a big-festival win is better than a prize from a small festival, at the end of the day, an award is an award. The idea behind this way of thinking is that no matter how small the festival, the more you can enter, the better your odds of winning a prize — and a project with awards from a small festival is always better than a project with no awards. I often ride the fence on both of these ideas, and make judgments based on the size of my project.

Home-Video Distribution

Options for home-video distribution are more plentiful today than they've ever been. From analog tape to digital discs to completely digital content, here is a brief outline of the life of home video, followed by how it all pertains to realistic distribution opportunities.

VHS is an acronym for "Video Home System" and "Vertical Helical Scan." Whatever the letters stand for, VHS is now a dying breed. The digital age has taken hold, and never have so many formats been vying for home-entertainment consideration. From single- and dual-layer DVD to Blu-ray and HD DVD, your options are growing year by year. As with all technological advances, this creates both benefits and pitfalls.

VHS's inevitable replacement, the DVD (digital video disc, or digital versatile disc), has had a long run of popularity around the globe. This is still the standard format of choice for most content creators, although new emerging technologies will push DVD out. Even older formats such as VHS have struggled to hang on through the creation of alternative versions — such as Super-VHS, Data-VHS, and even VHS-W — that can hold analog video in high definition. Yet despite VHS's fight for survival, the Motion Picture Association of America (MPAA) recently announced that movies will no longer be available on the older format.

Although the 1980s saw the first intense format war between JVC's VHS and Sony's Betamax, ultimately the longer recording time of VHS was a large contributing factor to the success of that format. This raises interesting questions when pondering the HD-format war: Sony's Blu-

Table 10-2 *The evolution of home-video formats*

Format	Capacity
Betamax	N/A (linear tape)
VHS	N/A (linear tape)
DVD	4.7 GB
Superbit DVD	4.7 GB
DVD dual layer	8.5 GB
HD DVD	15 GB–30 GB
Blu-ray	25 GB–50 GB
HVD (holographic versatile disc)	300 + GB

ray versus Toshiba's HD DVD. Blu-ray can hold nearly twice as much data as HD DVD (50 GB versus 30 GB, respectively). Although far more film studios back Blu-ray (see Table 10-3), many believe that as HD fully replaces DVD, Sony will have a leg up with dual-layer 50 GB titles.

Table 10-3 *Studio format support as of 2007*

Blu-ray	HD DVD
Paramount Pictures	Paramount Pictures
Warner Bros.	Warner Bros.
New Line Cinema	New Line Cinema
Columbia Pictures	Universal Studios
MGM	Weinstein Company
Disney	
20th Century Fox	
Sony Pictures	

Although many action-sports projects are already shipping with HD playback options (see Figure 10-3), the majority of them still ship on standard DVD. This is in large part because of the low cost of DVD duplication. Some projects are even being duplicated and printed at home now. DVD duplicators that can burn 5, 10, or even 100 copies from your master have become increasingly available on resale locations such as eBay. If you own a LightScribe or an ink-jet CD/DVD printer (available in most standard electronics stores), you can even print your discs with a professional finish.

If you plan to distribute low quantities of your movie among friends or even online, then this latter option may be ideal for you. Although the costs of replacement ink cartridges remain high for most printers, the overall ease of printing and burning from home can make it a great option for regular content creators.

Figure 10-3 Todd Seligman shooting Danny Way at the Great Wall in HD.

Many content creators now opt to shoot as much HD as possible, knowing that their projects will have a greater street value with distributors if they can offer them on standard-definition (SD) DVD as well as high-definition Blu-ray and HD-DVD. If you are just now in the planning stages of shooting your project, then try contacting some distribution companies that look right for you, and ask them about their desire for HD content. This may help to shape what format you shoot and how you finish your project.

You will find that some distributors are less concerned with format and more concerned with content. If you've shot top athletes in a sport or have a truly compelling and unique story, then you have a leg up on getting your project distributed. These are negotiating points that you'll want to bring up when going for the best deal. Oftentimes distribution companies will also want to know if you have plans to market the project yourself or if you have connections to get articles written about it. Although they likely have all of these connections themselves, and on some films will even spend their own dollars on advertising, anything you can bring to the table will also help to guarantee a slot in their lineup.

Illustration 10-2 DVD duplication quantities.

Home-video distribution deals will vary greatly as well, depending on the size of your project. Profit splits will usually come after any hard costs such as duplication have been recouped — and even then, the split can vary from as high as 70/30 in your favor to the exact opposite split in their favor. This latter split is more likely if your video has risks involved. Perhaps you can't promise any promotions of the project, so the distributor will have to front all the costs of advertising. Or maybe you don't have top riders in the video, and thus they don't know if it'll sell well enough to warrant doing minimum duplication requirements (typically 2,500 units). There are countless more reasons why profit splits can float far in either direction from a 50/50 deal. If you can, talk to someone who has dealt with your distribution company in the past, or do further research on the titles they've released, and consider how yours compares.

With all the competing formats and various unknowns regarding distribution, if you're new to the game or just unsure of which way to invest your time and money, then consider this: just as many home players are now combo units with VHS and DVD built in, expect to see inexpensive combo HD DVD and Blu-ray players. You don't have to make a decision on all of the technology now because it's going to take time for these devices to truly saturate the market. DVD is still the reigning format by choice, and it'll be some time before it goes away.

Figure 10-4
Holographic-disc technology. Courtesy Piotr Jaworski.

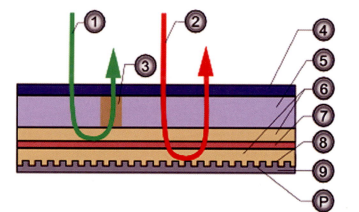

Holographic Versatile Disc structure
1. Green writing/reading laser (532 nm)
2. Red positioning/addressing laser (650 nm)
3. Hologram (data)
4. Polycarbon layer
5. Photopolymeric layer (data-containing layer)
6. Distance layers
7. Dichroic layer (reflecting green light)
8. Aluminium reflective layer (reflecting red light)
9. Transparent base
P. PIT

HVD (holographic versatile discs) are thought to be the absolute future of media. These optical discs have a theoretical capacity of 3.9 terabytes,[1] which is approximately 830 times the capacity of a DVD. Beginning with disc formats of 200 GB and 300 GB, HVDs begin shipping in 2008, but will take some time to become a staple of the industry. Whereas Blu-ray and HD DVD use blue lasers to write media to a disc, HVDs use a blue-green laser to write in a three-dimensional space in the disc. The high transfer rates and enormous storage capacities of HVDs will eventually make them ideal for the high-data-rate needs of video-content creators.

To put HVD capability in perspective, the U.S. Library of Congress has more than 130 million items in it. If scanned as text, the entire Library of Congress would fit on just six HVDs. In the world of iPods, that amounts to more than 20,000 hours of video (that's more than two years' worth). So when it comes to shooting, backing up, and distributing your HD content, HVD is the next logical step.

Until HVD takes off, however, a good DVD-distribution deal will help pay for your project. Because discs cost less than a dollar to duplicate in high quantity, if you're selling them online from your own web site for $10 a copy, you stand to make some money. In major stores, most films sell for about $20, and distributors sell them to the stores for around $10 to $12 each. Subtracting the hard costs of making the DVDs, a 50/50 split would yield you around $4 to $5 each. You might make less per disc than doing it yourself, but you'll likely be selling more discs this way.

Theatrical

It is only the occasional action-sports video that finds its way into movie theaters. Typically, these videos are documentary formatted, and feature the more popular or mainstream action sports, such as snowboarding, surfing, and skateboarding. These action-sports films are also usually accompanied by large budgets and high production value. A few top

---

[1] A terabyte is 1,024 gigabytes or 1 trillion bytes.

Table 10-4 *Action-sports documentaries released in movie theaters*

Theatrical action-sports videos	Sport featured	Year released	# of U.S. theaters	U.S. theatrical gross ($ million, est.)
First Descent	Snowboarding	2005	238	0.8
Dust to Glory	Baja 1000	2005	80	0.7
Riding Giants	Surfing	2004	64	2.4
Step into Liquid	Surfing	2003	91	3.7
Ultimate X	All sports	2002	48	4.2
Dogtown and Z-Boys	Skateboarding	2001	45	1.3

videos (see Table 10-4) to have graced the silver screen in the past decade went on to also be top sellers on DVD in the home-video market. In many ways, this is because theatrical releases have changed in goal and structure since the 1990s.

In the 1990s, most movies would gross more money in theaters than they would on home video. Today, home video far outgrosses theatrical. This is in part because so many people have surround-sound entertainment systems with high-resolution big-screen TVs. The result is that many theatrical films act as advertising campaigns for home video. Even though the prestige of getting your project into theaters still exists today, the real goal for many directors/producers is simply to get it out there, whether that means your film is seen in theaters or becomes a best-selling DVD.

Action sports, just like Hollywood movies, have been evolving and changing in the scope of what can get into theaters. Each year, movie studios are producing fewer big-budget movies for theatrical release, while simultaneously increasing the budgets of the few that they do. This is because movie theaters represent the last great outlet for pure entertainment spectacle (more on this in Chapter 12, The Future of Action-Sports Filmmaking). Big-budget, effects-laden summer movies still play better on the big screen. And this holds true for visual, high-production-value action-sports projects. Consider *Riding Giants*. What better place to see humans get towed in on surfboards at high speed to 50-foot waves than on the big screen? This is also true for heartwarming and compelling stories that transcend cultural niches such as action sports. In the case of *Dogtown and Z-Boys*, the real-life story of the birth of Venice Beach skateboarding, viewers were so intrigued by the characters and documentary footage that Hollywood hired top-name actors to portray the characters in the movie version, *Lords of Dogtown*.

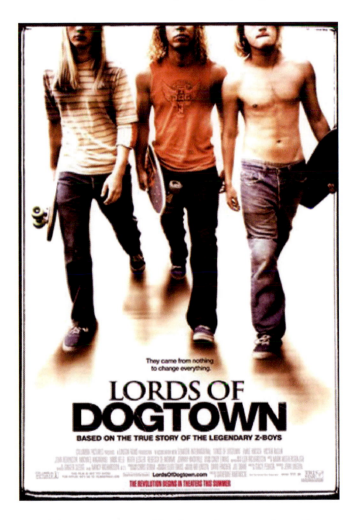

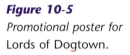

Figure 10-5
Promotional poster for Lords of Dogtown.

If your goal is to get your film into theaters, then there are a few simple steps you'll need to follow. First, if possible, make sure and shoot on HD or film. Theatrical screens project images that are approximately 2 K in size (see Chapter 2 for details), so you'll need to have the highest-quality image possible to play well in theaters. Although the occasional DV film will release in theaters (such as *The Blair Witch Project* and *28 Days Later*), the quality is noticeably degraded, and distributors will be reluctant to accept your project. Second, you're going big now, so make sure you have every single aspect of your project cleared: from music and talent clearances to locations and appearing logos. Finally, decide if your greatest asset is that you have large-title sponsors, big-name athletes, or that unique story (the way *Lords of Dogtown* does).

Compelling stories that would do well at film festivals are better off going out and winning awards before you pitch distributors. If you think you have a project that is worthy of an X-Dance — or even Sundance — win, then you may want to hold off on trying to sell your project until after it runs the festival circuit. On the other hand, if you were able to land sponsorship or get some top-name athletes, then you will need to put a solid press kit together to send out to distribution companies. Some distributors won't accept unsolicited material. This means that if you're just an individual, and your project doesn't have a sales agent or any type of representation, then you may want to consider going after an agent first. Here, the ideal way in is through a friend of a friend or any connection you can foster. A final outlet for getting your project out there is through online submissions. Various companies such as Netflix do in fact now fund and distribute some theatrical projects, so getting in with one of these companies can be a great asset.

Distribution at a theatrical level can be one of the hardest steps in content creation and exhibition. If you don't wind up getting that hundred-screen guarantee, or even one screen, don't sweat it. Home video really is becoming the prominent source for entertainment. The truth is, theatrical distribution for action sports can be very risky, and the last thing you probably want is for your project not to be profitable.

Television and Internet

On October 12, 2005, the Apple iTunes Store added support for buying and downloading video content. Then, on September 12, 2006, they

Figure 10-6 Apple
iTunes 7 video library.
Courtesy Apple.

increased the resolution of their content from 320 × 240 to the broadcast-size 640 × 480. These are major steps toward the future of home-video distribution. Once high-speed, real-time HD digital video files can be sent over the Internet on a regular basis, you and other content creators may no longer need to worry about duplication costs. It also means that some distributors of action-sports content will no longer need to worry about how many titles they take on. As a perfect example, look at online sites such as YouTube, which surpassed 6 million clips online in 2007, and was then growing at a rate of 65,000 new clips a day.

Posting your content online for downloadable and streaming file-sharing views has become the easiest way to distribute your material. File-sharing sites track view numbers. As your clip becomes more and more popular, you'll be able to identify exactly how many people are watching it and how they're rating it. In the past, these types of statistics were extremely difficult, if not impossible, to obtain. Using video online as an outlet to get distribution can also work today. Although the possibilities are endless, there are many approaches to doing it. Consider posting several sections of your work online to track, and later showing results to a potential investor, sponsor, or distributor. This would mean that you could create an online following through a vlog (video blog) or other site that you could use as leverage to get your next project green-lit.

Illustration 10-3
Television vs. the Internet.

In the past, the major networks controlled most of what viewers saw, but that power is shifting. The billions of dollars spent on advertising for broadcast is slowly dropping as fewer viewers tune in on a regular basis to conventional TV. With TiVo and DVRs in general, many of those who still watch TV regularly simply record their favorite shows and fast-forward past the commercials. In many respects, as the viewers shift onto the Internet, so will the advertising revenue, which will help create and spawn new Internet innovations, which will pull in more viewers, and so on. The snowball effect becomes cataclysmal as it approaches a definitive tipping point in which more viewers will be watching content online than on TV. With higher-speed bandwidth constantly developing, the Internet will eventually just absorb television as we know it today. Already, most popular TV shows have a web site where fans can watch episodes, interviews with stars, and even outtakes.

Just as filmmakers used to access footage linearly on tape and edit on tape-to-tape machines, now it's an instant-access, all-the-time nonlinear process. In that same way, television streams linearly just like the tapes of the past. But that all-access nonlinear version of content sharing is right around the corner, and it's the Internet. There are distribution companies that still sell shows and content to fill available television-broadcasting slots. Ironically, if you're interested in getting your project on TV, you can look up many of these companies online.

Perhaps you're shooting a documentary on a classic surf location, or even a ski resort with an incredible history. Then odds are, you might want to sell the broadcast rights to your video for TV, and then the home-video rights for DVD. If you have no intention of selling the rights to your project for any standard-distribution outlet, then maybe the Internet is the perfect home for it. Just know that even the toughest content encryption can and does get cracked. Programs exist to download content from YouTube and other video-sharing sites. People file-share and embed each other's content on their own sites. These facts are important to remember because if your project enters the world as a digital file, you take the chance that the moment you put it out there, it may never come home.

Alternate Outlets

The Internet may be your best start, but if you want to make your money back on a video, then consider alternate revenue outlets. A few popular ones include repurposing your video segments as cell-phone content; selling the original footage to a stock content house; perhaps posting your video in segments on a web site for free, and then using

Google AdWords or another company to place pay-per-click banner ads on your site; or even just flat-out selling the rights for your film to a production company for a flat rate.

All of these outlets and more are constantly evolving as technology changes. New cell-phone companies pop up, someone buys them, a web site spins out of it, and so on. The best way to track the changes and stay up-to-date on what's happening is online. Popular web sites such as Digg.com and Engadget.com — and even social-bookmarking sites such as del.icio.us — all track up-to-date trends as these technologies mature. One of the first revenue-sharing web sites for online video posting, Revver.com, now has countless competitors in that field alone. There are hundreds of options that have risen out of the Internet and because of cell phones. It wasn't that long ago that action-sports videos were being sold only on VHS. As overwhelming as it may be to have so many possibilities today, trust me — it's a good problem to have.

Big-Set Production: An Overview

So you shoot action sports, or perhaps you used to shoot action sports, but now you're looking to move on or into something newer, possibly bigger. Many filmmakers continue into other aspects of production as they go. It's a huge industry, and there are countless outlets to get involved in. Whether you want to try stretching your legs by working on a large feature-film set, or you are going to make your own feature film with an action-sports theme, this chapter will give you a broad understanding of big-set production, and a few ways to break into it.

From the first silent black-and-white films to the cutting-edge 3-D technology poised to change the industry, the movie process on set has remained one of the few unchanged elements throughout the years. Film sets can provide the ultimate learning environment for you. Don't just look at your time on set as learning about how to make movies — also look at it as a means to learn professional techniques and tricks that you can then take home and implement in your smaller projects. Everything you learn will be an enormous asset to your action-sports productions, so do your best to take it all in.

Film sets can range drastically in shapes and sizes. Even studio film shoots can include anywhere from a couple dozen to a few hundred people on set. Take the case of the summer action film *xXx* from Revolution Studios. There were days in which the cast and crew totaled only 40, but other times as many as several hundred. This is because scenes themselves vary so greatly in complexity. For example, large crews are

Figure 11-1 A large
film set.

needed for a huge scene with explosions, loads of extras, enormous lighting setups, and massive sets — but then not for a small conversation on a beach between two people.

If you've ever been on a large movie set, then chances are you know how hectic it can seem — various departments all moving in different directions as if it were total chaos. Yet somehow everyone seems to know exactly what to do and when to do it. It can really be quite impressive to watch.

My first experience on a movie set was for *Batman & Robin,* with George Clooney and Arnold Schwarzenegger. We were shooting at Warner Bros. on their largest soundstage. My first day there, I saw a hundred people all moving about, and I couldn't understand what they could possibly be doing. As I wandered inside, the outer walls of the set were unfinished two-by-fours, sheets of plywood, pipes, and so on. It didn't look impressive. Then I stepped through a doorway and into a room so large and incredible it suddenly all made sense: an enormous re-created museum that had massive columns, a huge lighting rig

Table 11-1 *Key departments on a big summer-movie production*

• Production assistants (PAs)	Entry-level position, typically assist the ADs
• Armory	Handle weapons such as guns and blank ammo
• Art department	Production and set designers
• Camera department	Operators, focus pullers, film loaders, etc.
• Casting	Responsible for finding and casting talent
• Catering	Meals
• Construction	Building/executing set construction
• Director and assistant directors	Usually a 1st AD and a 2nd AD work for director
• Grip	Lighting and rigging technicians (e.g., dolly grip)
• Greens	Trees, shrubs, grass, flowers, etc.
• Lighting and electric	Electricians and a gaffer set up lights
• Locations	Scouting, finding, locking filming locations
• Props	Finding, making, and providing all on-set props
• Makeup/hair	Talent hair and/or makeup stylists
• Script supervisor/continuity	Tracks each shot with the script for continuity
• Set decorating	Dresses the film set
• Sound	Booming and mixing all sound on set
• Special-effects department	Handles all on-set effects such as smoke and fire
• Stunt department	2nd unit director, stunt coordinators, and stuntmen
• Technical advisers	Unique subject experts used for guidance on set
• Transportation	Cars and trucks for cast, crew, and equipment
• Visual-effects department	Supervise shoot to better incorporate VFX later
• Wardrobe	All costumes for talent

suspended from the ceiling, and a hardworking crew polishing every last detail of the set to create an immense reality the way only movies can. All of the crew members that I saw were working for key departments, each of which had a specific number of personnel working to achieve their specific goal. Table 11-1 shows a breakdown of a typical film's crew and department list.

If you want to get involved but you don't know anyone, stuntmen can sometimes be the easiest to get to know, especially if you're an athlete. Most stuntmen come from unique backgrounds such as martial arts, car racing, or even action sports. They operate as a tight group, working with their peers and watching out for each other's safety.

Feature films may seem overwhelming if you're new to them, but like the stunt team, each department operates on its own as a small, unique team of experts in that category. They will interact closely only with other departments that directly relate to what they're doing. For example, the camera department is led by the cinematographer, and thus they interact with lighting and grip, but rarely does a cameraman need to speak with makeup or locations. In addition, the lower you are on the totem pole of that department, the more isolated and focused your work may be. A camera or film loader — who is responsible for making sure that all film magazines are loaded, organized, and ready to go — may spend very little time at all on set if he's busy loading and dropping new film magazines off to the ACs (assistant cameramen). In fact, a film loader's interaction may be limited just to the ACs.

If you have shot action sports and are trying to get involved in movie production, or perhaps there's a film on snowboarding shooting near your hometown, then you may be able to get involved and learn more by applying to be a PA (production assistant) or personal assistant. Oftentimes crews will travel with only their key personnel, and then hire locals to help with the more basic tasks on location. If a movie is coming to your town, either contact your local city hall or look up the movie on the IMDB[1] and see if the production company is listed, then send them a résumé and email asking how to get involved.

As a personal assistant, you might be responsible for getting the director coffee, or working with a producer on and off set to make sure they can do their job in your town. PAs usually get a little bit more on-set action, but that job has a wide range of duties as well. Some people have amazing PA experiences — working with cast, ADs (assistant directors), or just helping on set. Others have less-exciting experi-

---

[1] The Internet Movie Database has the largest online database of films (IMDB.com).

ences — helping to stop traffic all day from a corner nowhere near the set. A unique way into the business is as a writer. By this route, you can spend all your time at home, possibly never even on or even near a set. Scripts now have festivals as well (see Withoutabox.com for a partial list), so it's easier to get discovered as a first-time writer. Then, as a successful writer, you can slowly make the transition to directing, if that's your goal.

This is what makes the film business so exciting. Every production and every day of every production is different. You never know what you're going to get, so by jumping in feet first with enthusiasm and motivation, you set yourself up to learn, make connections, and begin to climb the ladder in Hollywood.

Figure 11-2 *On the set of director Bill Kiely's Vans commercial with Bucky Lasek.*

So you've decided to make your first large project. Perhaps you've got a rich uncle, or maybe you've written a script on action sports and you're going to raise the money. However you've gotten your financing, here are some key steps to consider as you move forward. First off, you aren't the first to make an independent film, so the best place to start is with those who have come before you. We always hear about the self-financed small films that make it big: *Napoleon Dynamite, My Big Fat Greek Wedding,* and *The Blair Witch Project,* to name a few. But what we never hear about are the countless productions that never make it to the screen — or, worse yet, to the edit bay. There are heaps of online independent-filmmaking web sites that offer forums, bulletins, and articles on the successful and unsuccessful paths of those who have walked before you. From indieWIRE.com to FilmTies.com, you'll find countless sites devoted to independent filmmaking. The key is to do your homework to best ensure the success of your project.

The second thing to remember is that most action-sports videos sell to enthusiasts of their respective sport. If you plan on making a feature film with action sports, and hope that mainstream audiences will enjoy it, then you'll need a mainstream story. Nobody goes to see *Happy Gilmore* with Adam Sandler because they love golf. The film's positives — a good story, good actors, and fulfilling character arcs — are enough. This holds true for many films, but unfortunately, most action-sports narrative films that have come before us have all focused heavily on the "extreme" sports aspect of their movie instead of the story. So if you plan to make a feature film, without or even with action sports involved, make sure you keep your story and characters as the focus.

Your next big goal will be to start preproduction. This will include building your crew and making the creative decisions that will shape the world you're going to shoot. Large-scale productions are put together by a producer and a line producer. If this is your creative project, then you should be focusing on directing. Don't worry about the daunting task of building your crew; instead, find someone you trust to handle that aspect. If you don't know where to begin, go online and find an experienced producer who can build your crew for you. That is their job, and on a large project, you shouldn't be worrying about that aspect

Figure 11-3 *Shooting pro skateboarder Danny Way, downtown Los Angeles.*

anyway. Producers are responsible for hiring most of the key crew, and for working closely with the line producer to find crew and manage the budget of the movie. Together, these two positions are the basis for getting everything to the set that's needed. It's then up to you, working with your crew, to assemble the pieces into your vision.

Set Etiquette

The director may be the point of the sword on any movie set, but it is always up to you to act professionally and properly while on set. Set etiquette will vary greatly depending on what position of the crew or cast you are filling. Here are a few simple tricks and techniques to maintaining proper set etiquette.

If you're visiting a set for the first time, remember this: things move fast and inconsistently. If you've ever visited an assembly shop or machine room, you've seen the precision repetition of the process. So-and-so picks up such and such, moves it here, gets another, repeats. On movie sets, everything is always changing, and no one has any one repeatable path — so keep your eyes open. From carrying light stands to moving set cars, you can find yourself very quickly in the way of the flow. No one on a crew knows when they'll be in the way either, so it's nothing to worry over if it happens once or twice, but don't get so immersed in a conversation or camera you brought that you fail to notice the three guys pushing a crane your way. You'll hear expressions such as "Hot points coming through!" — which simply means that something sharp or pointed (say, a tripod) is headed right at you.

You'll also notice that most crew members tend to either be on the move working, or just sitting around. This is where the expression "hurry up and wait" comes from. On the set of movies, you aren't always needed — but when you are, you need to be ready. So the idea is that you can sit there and chat all day long if there's nothing to be done — but when you hear your name or department called, you move immediately. You'll notice that most crew members have earpieces for their walkie-talkies as well. This can make for an interesting first experience when you're talking to someone, and they suddenly look away and walk off. It's understood in production that when you are called, you go. If everyone finished up the conversation before going back to work, films would never get made.

Another key approach to being on set is to keep your back against something solid. A good choice would be a wall. If you stand out of the way against a wall (one that isn't in the shot, of course), then you'll more than likely be in the safest place possible. Out-of-the-way corners are great spots to quietly observe and get the feel for the set. As mentioned, every day and every set is different, so even if the filmmakers are having a great time one moment, things could be going wrong the next — and you never want to be the one in the line of fire.

I spent six months living in Australia in the winter of 2004, working on the production of *Stealth*. We shot a great deal on soundstages, then moved into the Blue Mountains outside Sydney. On an unusually windy day, we were shooting in a deep valley near a stream. Everything was going fine, and the production seemed calm and typical of any other day — when a giant gust of wind came barreling down the valley wall. We had a large white cloth reflector tied off in a metal frame on stands. The reflector was restrained for safety atop a large rock. But Mother

Nature has a way of letting you know who's in charge. With next to no warning, that reflector said *hasta la vista* to the sandbags as it started to take flight. Like any respectable crew member, the nearest grip grabbed hold to secure the reflector — only to take off with it. Not possessing the aeronautical design of even a Wright brothers' test, the reflector pretty much went earthbound and took that brave grip with it. A couple feet of water from the stream broke his fall, and he came up soaked and okay, with eight lives remaining. This was a huge crew well versed in production, and even then, random things like this can happen. The lesson here was twofold: keep your eyes wide open and your feet on the ground.

Figure 11-4 *Stage 5, Fox Studios Australia, outside Sydney.*

Finally, if you've been hired to work on the set and you're a bit unfamiliar with procedures, consider the following summary of basic principles that apply on most new jobs and are key on film sets. First, show up on set early. Make sure you're there before your actual call time. From finding crew parking to waiting for a transport van to drive you to the set, you'll just make a better impression and be more relaxed if you get there early. Next, most crew members are friendly and outgoing, so be polite; say hello; and, most importantly, introduce yourself and find out what they do. If you're not good at remembering names, then come up with a trick that works for you. Crews can be large, and you may run into and/or be working with these people, so get to know them by name. Third, you'll want to be motivated and focused but also humble. Nobody likes a know-it-all, and you're part of a team now, so focus on your job and your department. Keep your ears open for someone to call out your name or those of fellow department members. Lastly, don't be afraid to ask questions. If you don't know something, ask. Most crews are happy to share and explain how something works. Just try not to ask anyone who's in the middle of working. The members of your own department are best for questions because you don't want to disturb or bother the wrong person by accident (such as the director).

Networking

So you're on set working with a big crew, and now you want to network. One of the best ways to get future jobs in the film business is to be referred by someone in the business. Many cameramen will work their entire lives for the same DP (director of photography) once they get in. They may start as a film loader, then climb to a second AC, then first AC (or focus puller), than eventually an operator or even DP. A good friend and longtime industry cameraman, Richard Merryman, has shot more than 25 movies. He got his start as a film loader. In 1981, Richard met Oscar-winning cinematographer Dean Semler and went on to work for Dean on all his movies. I first met Richard and Dean in 2001 during preproduction on *xXx*. At the same time, I met a talented young producer, Amy Wilkes, who was on set with her husband, Rich, who had written *xXx*. After becoming friends, Amy produced a short film for me, which Richard shot, called *Men of Action* (see Figure 11-5). Dean offered enormous help by arranging our cameras for us. Our friendship began on set, which is how you'll meet many of the people that you might spend your career working with on various projects.

Figure 11-5 *On the set of* Men of Action *with Richard Merryman. Photo by Chris Mitchell.*

If you're on a movie for any great length of time, you should make friends naturally. However, if you're on for only a week or two, and you want to network and try to make some new connections in the industry, then here are a few tips. First, you should pick a department to network with that is of true interest to you. If you want to be a cameraman, then meet the loaders, talk to them, and see if they'll introduce you to the cameramen or DP. It's crucial, though, that you don't disturb the director — or anyone else, for that matter — while they're working. A good time to introduce yourself or say hello is in the morning, when everyone is just settling in. Usually by the end of the day, the director and others are rushing out to screen dailies — or they have meetings, and the film is still on their minds. You'll find during shooting that there are occasional breaks, and if you watch the director or others closely, you can observe when they are working (which includes thinking), and when they are not. If they appear to be out of work mode, and you can catch them for a moment, then a polite introduction and hello is usually fine. You can even express your level of interest and motivation to learn more. Many great filmmakers got started by volunteering themselves or interning to learn the ropes. There may not be any money in it, but the wealth of knowledge and relationships can be invaluable. While I was in college, my first real gig was interning nights at a company called T-Bone Films in Santa Monica. Doing tape-to-tape edits for filmmaker Evan Stone and producer Craig Caryl was a great stepping-stone to the world of production.

Another option to network and meet new crew members can be the wrap party for any one project. If you've been working especially hard and have been very punctual, then chances are you've made numerous overworked crew members' lives a little easier. When you approach them, be polite, as always. Ask them this: if you ever have any questions, could you stay in touch? You can let them know you would like to work with them again. Request that they call you if they ever need help on anything. Chances are, if you shone on set, you'll get a call.

Shooting Behind the Scenes

Well, it's officially standard on just about every film now. And one of the easiest ways to get feature-film-set experience that you can use on your action-sports projects is by shooting behind the scenes. The "making of" has become a staple of movie sets, and the opportunities for action-sports cameramen and documentarians to get onto big sets are expanding. In the years before DVD extras, there would be only a set photographer shooting stills for publicity, and an occasional EPK (electronic press kit) crew getting bits for television promotion or archival purposes. Today, Hollywood films will spend upwards of hundreds of thousands of dollars on creating and documenting the process. This comes in large part because of the added value (literally) of DVDs. As home-video technology continues to expand (see Chapter 10, Distribution), the ability to create more and more extra content will grow, as will consumer expectations.

From interactive-menu design and featurettes to online viral campaigns and commentaries, behind-the-scenes work on films has never been growing as quickly as it is right now. Top content creators still exist as large companies, but countless small film productions hire independent videographers to shoot their projects. By getting involved with a larger company, or trying to get on several small films to get the ball rolling, you can carve out a niche for yourself while observing and learning the craft of feature filmmaking.

Figure 11-6 On set and behind the scenes.

All of the previously discussed rules of set etiquette still apply, but when you're on set shooting behind the scenes, you'll spend much more time floating around between departments than you will sitting still. A typical "making of" or EPK position will begin with your speaking to the producers of the movie and working out what you'll be doing and what the budget will be for it.

For smaller-budgeted independent features, there are two main jobs you can go after. The first job is that of just shooting the behind-the-scenes footage. Oftentimes the production company or studio behind the film will just want you to shoot, then hand over the tapes — they will handle editorial themselves. If this is the case, then you'll need to get a feel for what their schedule is like and how many days you'll be needed. You can start by asking them what their expectations are: did they hope you'd be on set every day, or are they planning on just having you out for a few days? If they're unsure, then consider the size of the budget and whether everyone is getting paid well on this shoot, or if it's a project on a really tight budget. If it's the latter, then you'll have to decide if you'd rather spend more days on set and get paid less, or work fewer days but make more. To find out the budget and how tight it is, you could ask a friend who might be working on the project, or you could be very open about it with the company or studio (or whoever is hiring you) and just come right out and ask. If you do decide to ask, explain to them that their answer will help you create a schedule and budget that will more likely work for them.

Your next step will be to sit down and develop a proposal. If you know the shoot is 28 days, and it's almost all dialogue in the same room, then you may not need to be on set every day. On the other hand, if the film travels all over the state, and almost every production day contains interesting material, then you may want to be there as many days as possible.

You'll definitely want to be there on all of the key days. These include days that feature big action, days when all the cast is on set, days with important plot points, and so on. You can ask for a current shooting schedule (called a one-line schedule) and a copy of the script to help you lay this all out. If you pitch yourself for nearly every day, consider what your cost of operation will be with any of your gear, then simply tally it all up. Just remember, though, that if you come up with a high day rate for yourself, then add on your camera, a sound person, and even general expenses, it can get quite costly, fast.

A final consideration for making your proposal will be format. As always, you need to pick what you'll shoot on. Although many big productions are interested only in HD (high definition) or HDV (high-definition video) nowadays, many small productions are less concerned and will settle for DV (digital video). Just keep in mind that you may have to rent gear to meet their format expectations, so this could affect your budget significantly.

If you've been hired to shoot on set and to deliver final elements, then you have a few options on how to approach the job. If the company hasn't told you or doesn't know what elements they want for the DVD or promotional use, then you will have to pitch them on some ideas of your own. Although some companies will ask for a ten-minute featurette on the making of their film and perhaps a few other extras (see Table 11-2), most companies aren't sure, and thus will be open to your ideas. If this is the case, then you should take the script home to read and have a few good brainstorming sessions on what you could do for it. Remember to be realistic in your proposals, though, so you don't wind up promising more than you can deliver.

Figure 11-7 *The "making of": director Rob Cohen walks with Jeffrey Kimball. Photo by Jesse Kaplan.*

227

Table 11-2 *Popular DVD extras elements for feature films*

Popular elements	Approximate length
"Making of" featurette	3–90 minutes (average piece: 15 minutes)
Director or cast commentary	Duration of movie
Outtakes or bloopers	3–5 minutes (music driven)
Cast/crew bios	text (1–3 pages each)
Element-specific featurette	5–20 minutes
Behind-the-music featurette	3–10 minutes
Deleted scenes	2–8 scenes

Once you've read the script and thought about it, consider what's unique to this project and which elements stand out. If there's a horror element, then a featurette on doing all the special effects and makeup might be interesting. If there's a strong action-sports element, then a piece on action sports and who's involved would be great. Just think outside the box, and even consider web spots that you could make for them.

When you get the job and arrive on your first day of shooting, you'll want to find the ADs first off and introduce yourself. Before you even consider shooting, it's always wise to make sure that the key people know who you are. ADs are responsible for running the set, so if you're supposed to be there, and they're aware of you, then you're good to go. If you can, try to introduce yourself to as many people as possible before you roll. Begin with the director, who, like many people on the set, may not want to be shot. It's a common courtesy that will make your day go much more smoothly. Even find time to say hello to the actors and help make them feel comfortable with you. As everyone becomes more open to you and your camera, you will get better material.

Use many of the camera techniques discussed in Chapters 5 and 6. Begin wide and far out, then slowly work your way in as people become more comfortable with your shooting them. Also find a nice balance of time when you are shooting and time when you are not shooting. This will give the cast and crew a break from the camera. No one likes to be filmed all the time. The best way to handle this can sometimes be to take an "out of sight, out of mind approach." When you're not shooting, try to fade back into the shadows, or put down the camera and just give people a mental break. It's not only about whether or not you're filming. If you're standing there holding the camera at your side while everyone works, just by seeing you, they may feel like they're keeping their guard up. You'll make everyone's day if you make things fun, easy, and painless for them.

Figure 11-8 *Over-the-shoulder shots.*

When you're on set shooting, you may not want to cover every take. Some directors may do up to ten takes, and your video camera can also affect the actors' comfort zone. So try keeping your distance on takes until you know they are cool with it — and even then, never stand in an actor's eye line while the movie is filming. If it's an important scene, cover the 10 different takes from numerous angles. Capture the director watching one, then film the actors, then get a wide master, and so on. If the scene isn't that important, don't feel that you have to shoot every take; you'll just be kicking yourself later when you scan through hours of repeating footage. On the other hand, be careful not to miss that outtake on Take 32. If you do miss something, don't worry. Shots can get missed; it's the nature of the game.

Some standard shots you can go for during takes include shooting over the director's shoulder so you see the film set and his monitor (see Figure 11-8). Also try getting shots from behind the cameramen's perspective, thus showing what they're shooting (see Figure 11-9). In general, you want to stay out of people's way both physically and mentally, while still getting in there to capture the best shots possible. It's a delicate balance.

Figure 11-9 Behind the cameraman on set. Photo by Chris Mitchell.

How many tapes should you shoot? If you're covering every day of a long production, and you have a good sense of what you want, need, and are capable of getting, then I find that one to two hours of tape is a good average. If you weren't sure of any of the above, then I'd roll more to be on the safe side. If you're there for only a few days of the entire shoot, then you're going to want to get as much as possible. This doesn't mean shoot the same take from the same angle repeatedly, but rather, get creative and see how different you can make everything look. If you're the only one filming on set, then you should mix up your shooting style for possible other pieces down the road. Capture a take of a scene slowly, starting wide and zooming in patiently, then do another take with a completely opposite approach. This time, make the camera moves frenetic; crash-zoom in and land on a Dutched angle of the actor. The goal is to create options in post. Shooting these days can result in five to ten tapes. When you wrap on your assignment, if you're just delivering tapes, find out if they want them at the end of the shoot or the end of every day; with the latter, you won't have the responsibility of holding them for a month. When I created the *xXx* "making of," I was overnighting boxes of shot tapes back to LA from the Czech Republic every few weeks.

If you're doing post as well, you may need to dive right into it. Once you know what elements have been approved, you'll want to start logging your footage as soon as you can. Behind-the-scenes shooting can result in lots of footage, so quickly getting a handle on it will help you achieve your edits. Expect to turn in rough cuts to the production company for approval, and make sure you have a prenegotiated number of allowed changes. Otherwise you could wind up doing far more work in post than you had ever planned.

Behind-the-scenes shooting is a great way to take what you already know about action-sports or documentary shooting, and parlay it into some on-set experience. This can really be perfect for establishing that knowledge base and for making connections in the world of feature filmmaking.

Commercials, Music Videos, and Short Films

If you plan to shoot something locally for a friend, an online competition, or even just for yourself, start by trying to put a good production team together from everyone you know. If you have friends who are ready and willing to help out, even if they don't know the process themselves, get them involved and teach them what you know. Making films and videos can be a very fun but difficult task, so usually the more help you can get, the better.

Figure 11-10
Documenting the Men of Action *"making of."* *Photo by Chris Mitchell.*

Commercial production is a changing world. As mentioned in Chapter 10, advertisers are beginning to shift their money from television to the Internet. No longer is the industry locked up and unreachable. In the past, companies would go only with advertising agencies and large commercial production houses. However, with the changing front of advertising, more and more webisodes and web commercials are being done on the cheap, and thus below the radar of these agencies. This opens doors for you and other content producers out there.

Local companies can now afford to promote their products more easily, thanks to online video. If you want to get your foot in the commercial door, then start with a few specs. A spec commercial is essentially a spot that you make on your own for a company that is in no way supporting you. Popular spec-commercial subjects have included beers, cars, and foods. In 2003, DP Bridger Nielson shot a KFC spec commercial with me for our reels (see Figure 11-11).

Although it is possible to sometimes contact an advertising agency and see if they have any unused or old storyboards for commercial spots, you can simply write your own spec. Come up with a unique concept that promotes the product and works around your existing assets. If you shoot Freestyle BMX primarily, then consider making a spec commercial for a Freestyle BMX industry product, or you might simply incorporate Freestyle BMX into your commercial for another product.

Essentially, spec commercials can be the best way to build a reel that you can then submit to local retailers, production companies, or even agencies. It can be hard or almost impossible to get going in any industry without prior experience. By making a few specs, you'll have the chance to show people your talent.

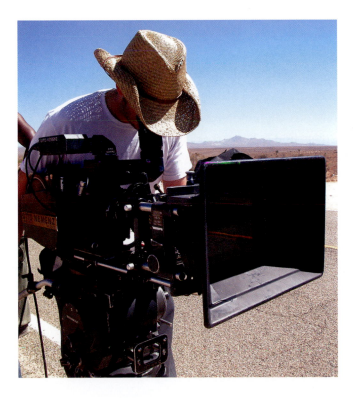

Figure 11-11 *KFC spec commercial shoot with DP Bridger Nielson.*

Other small projects that can allow you to stretch your creative legs include music videos. Pretty much anywhere in the country, you can find up-and-coming bands that would love to have a music video made. If you are interested in trying new projects and further honing your skills, then music videos can be a great way to do it.

Because of their nature, music videos are very often not linear stories. They may lack continuity and represent visual works of art. This allows for the widest range of creative expression, and can be far more forgiving when it comes time to edit. If your video is going to be a montage of the band's performance mixed in with images of an athlete cruising down a long, windy hill, then you can shoot it all without worries of what shot will go where. Although some videos can be completely scripted, many are simply conceptually designed and outlined, and then final decisions are made in post. This tactic will give you the greatest creative range. If you're shooting on a tight budget, you can be a little more carefree in your approach, less concerned for perfect lighting and continuity.

The subject of my first music video was a band called Slugg-O. A young director Sheldon Candis and I just set the band up in an alley in downtown Los Angeles. The band and their song were punk rock, so we decided that gritty and real would be our angle. We placed lights right in the shots and let them flare the lenses — it was great. Even hip-hop videos can be done with a fish-eye lens and a few creative locations. You should start by looking at what production equipment you have access to, then find a band that suits your taste. Post an ad online in your area on message boards for production and music (possibly on craigslist or MySpace). Once you start getting responses, talk to the bands about their expectations and your own, make sure you are both on the same page, and then begin to pitch ideas and concepts that you know you can make.

The key to a great video is your level of passion. Don't shoot a video for a song you don't like or can't relate to. Music videos reach out to people and often invoke an emotional response from the music and images, so make sure the song is powerful to you emotionally, and that you have a clear vision on how to portray that emotion with your camera.

Figure 11-12 On set in the Combi Bowl, Vans Skatepark. Courtesy Windowseat Pictures.

Commercials and music videos may allow you to disregard continuity, but when you're ready to practice your storytelling narrative abilities, the short film is a great place to turn. Most popular shorts have ranged anywhere from 1 to 20 minutes. It's tough to say what the ideal short-film length is. With user-generated content, television channels such as Current TV and web sites such as YouTube are now very popular. Many people love to tune in for 1- to 3-minute pieces.

If you plan to make a short, first you'll need a script. This can come from you or any of your friends. You can even go online to find sites for short scripts and search the entire planet for a good one. Next, you'll want to start filling in your cast and crew. In the past, I've shot various shorts that had as little as 1 cast member and 1 crew (see Figure 11-13), or as many as 60 people involved (see Figure 11-14). The deciding factor is really the content that you're shooting, and how "big" or "small" you want the production to be.

Figure 11-13 Short-film shoot with F. Valentino Morales, no crew.

Figure 11-14 Men of Action *short-film shoot, large cast and crew.*

The key to picking a crew size comes down to numerous factors. An important one includes the decision to shoot with or without permits. If you're going to get permits, as required by most state laws, they'll cost you some money and take time and paperwork. It can be as simple as calling your local parks and recreation department, if that's where you want to shoot, and asking what they'll require. If you decide to guerrilla your shoot, then just remember you're taking a chance, and any city official or owner of a private location has the right to ask you to leave. There are countless situations where you may never be bothered, including shooting with a very small crew, but I'd still advise finding out if you need permits and location releases for your shoot. Another factor for determining crew size can be how much time you want to spend shooting. If you have only an afternoon, contrary to the idea that more people can do more things, a big crew can actually slow you down. Being agile and mobile can save loads of time on set. As a director, you'll essentially have less to choose from when shooting, which makes things go faster. There are times when a well-thought-out, simple concept, can make for a great two-day weekend shoot. These are good "practice" shoots, chances to hone your skills. When you decide to go for broke and invest your money in a big short, then a bigger crew with more equipment and cast may be appropriate. Just use your best judgment on when that time is right.

Think of shorts, music videos, and even commercials all as ways to expand your filmmaking toolbox. There are constant crossover skills to the action-sports projects you will do, and in that world, you can use all of the tricks and techniques you learn. Some projects will be bigger, some smaller — but they're all still made with the same basic tools, beginning with you.

The Future of Action-Sports Filmmaking

12

One of America's truly famous artist and avant-garde[1] filmmakers, Andy Warhol, once said, "It's the movies that have really been running things in America ever since they were invented. They show you what to do, how to do it, when to do it, how to feel about it, and how to look how you feel about it."

There's a certain irony here, in that countless artists and filmmakers of today were themselves influenced and shaped by Andy's work. The truth is that media in totality provide a unique way for the world to communicate and know what others are up to. The visual arts of video, film, and digital media are a language, just like English or Japanese, and it's through this language that filmmakers share ideas and information with the world.

As an action-sports filmmaker, just like any other type of moviemaker, you are participating in these conversations by sharing your ideas and visions. Perhaps you are showing what tricks athletes are doing in your area, how the athletes are dressing, talking, or even how they greet each other with the constantly evolving handshake that people do. Action-sports filmmaking models itself after the sports it documents. The genre is ever evolving, growing, and finding balance with the expectations of those who watch it — and of those who do it.

---

[1] Avant-garde is a French term that refers to things — oftentimes films — that are artistic or experimental in nature.

Figure 12-1 Filmmaker
Chris Edmonds on
location. Photo by
Tim Peare.

There are many places action-sports filmmaking can go. Some of these places are more likely than others, but inevitably, the ultimate destination is unknown. In the constant race to create new projects and original ideas, it is critical to consider what has come before, and where other types of media are headed. To predict the future of action sports, we must first consider where we began.

How Far Can a Progressive Sport Go?

In 1985, not one person had ever done a backflip in competition on a vert ramp. By the '90s, skateboarders, Freestyle BMXers, and in-line skaters were all doing them. Then, by the early 2000s, as mentioned in

Chapter 1, professional snowboarder and in-line skater Matt Lindenmuth did the first ever double backflip on vert. This was followed by FMX legend Travis Pastrana's landing a double backflip on his dirt bike.

With current action-sports progression adding more rotations, bigger air, longer grinds, and mind-blowingly more-technical tricks, it's almost safe to say that the sky is no longer the limit. Although all sports have experienced enormous highs and lows in popularity since they first hit the scene, the action-sports industry as a whole has continued to grow over time. Let's consider skateboarding for a moment. In 1963, Larry Stevenson designed and sold the first professional skateboards (see Figure 12-2). At the time, skateboarding was just a "freestyle" activity, consisting of stylized turns and maneuvers. The following years were booming, and tens of millions of boards were sold. Then, out of nowhere, the industry collapsed in 1975, and skateboarding went underground. This put skaters back to the drawing board, which led to numerous tricks — including the Ollie — being invented. Although skateboarding slowly grew back into mainstream awareness, it died again — this time in 1991 with the U.S. recession. But by then, snowboarding was taking hold. This helped skateboarding grow back into public favor, along with in-line skating, which was at the time getting significant public attention. With action sports now growing in popularity, it was Tony Hawk's 900 at the X Games in 1999 (see Chapter 1) that caused the world to go ballistic.

Action sports were here to stay.

Every action sport has had similar ups and downs throughout the industry's relatively short life span, but it is worth noting the intense dues paid by snowboarding and skateboarding since their birth. This may account for their permanent fan base and place in the world today. The progressive nature of the sports will not change: new tricks will be invented, younger kids will someday outskate their idols, and new skate videos will find an audience.

If you plan to shoot another sport that is still going through growing pains, then consider the hills and valleys of the industries mentioned above, and how your action sport may be affected in the coming years.

Figure 12-2 *Larry Stevenson, skateboarding legend and inventor of the kick tail.*

A perfect example is in-line skating, which reached a low point in popularity in the early 2000s. Now that the sport is underground, in-line skating's anti-cool status has slowly been getting new kids involved — in large part for the same reasons that kids first took to snowboarding, freestyle skiing, and skateboarding: these new pursuits went against what was popular and mainstream.

One would think that there must come a point in all sports when, no matter what level of popularity they enjoy, there simply isn't anyplace left to go. The truth is that even when the well-established movie theater experience began to feel stale, back when surround sound felt like old news and Hollywood couldn't squeeze any more explosions into 90 minutes, along came 3-D. There may not be 3-D action-sports films out there yet, but why not? How much more intense would a 900 on a vert ramp or a grind down a handrail look in 3-D? Or maybe consider what you could do using your computer and various effects programs. You might be able to take an action-sports video to a new, creative place. As the ideas become old, new ones will always surface. Just as tricks will always progress, there's no reason the films shouldn't progress as well.

Figure 12-3 *Action Sports World Tour, Munich, Germany. Courtesy ASA Entertainment.*

Technology and the Future of Filmmaking

He gave us *The Terminator, Aliens,* and *Titanic.* In 2009, James Cameron's *Battle Angel* and *Avatar* mark the first in the wave of new digital 3-D technology to enter the big screen. The new polarized-glasses technology is far superior to the old blue and red glasses of the past. Theater chains continue to convert their projectors to digital systems that also handle 3-D, and the world awaits the spectacle and unique experience that new 3-D films will bring.

Yes, 3-D is the new frontier in taking theatrical experiences to the next level — and eventually home video as well. Even if you're making action-sports projects, these technologies will affect you. It's important to always keep an eye on the emerging technological front.

From his early days, even James Cameron has managed to keep one hand on technology, and the other on the heart of his projects: the stories. Jim Gianopulos, cochairman of Fox Filmed Entertainment, called James Cameron "not just a filmmaker," adding that "every one of his films have pushed the envelope in its aesthetic and in its technology."[2]

As this technology continues to expand and evolve around us, there will be countless new ways to embrace the production side of your projects, as well as the distribution. If 3-D cinema at the movies is a five-course meal, then that would make YouTube a PB and J — and most everyone loves both. Even two technologies from opposite ends of the spectrum still have enormous appeal to the same audience. In fact, when 3-D becomes a staple of big summer movies — just as HD has taken over from film cameras[3] — then who is to say that it won't trickle down in the coming years to the prosumer level.

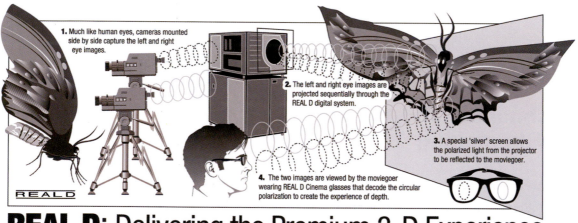

REAL D: Delivering the Premium 3-D Experience

Figure 12-4 Digital 3-D camera technology by REAL D.

[2] "Computers Join Actors in Hybrids On Screen," *New York Times*, January 9, 2007.

[3] Even though many DPs and directors still prefer film, more and more studio features are shot each year on high-end HD cameras.

In 2004, O'Reilly Media coined the phrase "Web 2.0," referring to the changing face of the Internet. No longer is the web a place to stare at 2-D pages full of data. Instead, it has evolved into a place were users generate and share information. People post their bios, videos, stills, and ideas online; they react and respond to other postings, thus creating a snowball effect of shared content and creation. This network of sharing means that even the two-dimensional video projects of the past will evolve as online distribution evolves. Perhaps your future project will not only allow, but also depend on, user interaction.

Top action-sports videos such as *411VM* video magazine already compile shots of tricks from numerous filmers all over the world. What if this were to happen automatically via a web site? Could a program be written to allow the top vote getters among user-posted clips to be automatically shuffled and placed into a video montage online? What if a program could even identify key "trick moments" as a way to sync each shot up to the recurring beats of the user-chosen song? These are just the beginning of the questions you need to ask yourself as filmmaking moves into the future. Three-dimensional digital technology, the internet as a means of sha content, and the creativity that only you can provide — these are building blocks of tomorrow's films and videos. What they'll become when put together will shape the future of the industry.

You Read the Book . . . Now What?

Whether you're new to filmmaking or you've been shooting your whole professional life, chances are you are reading this book because you're serious about expanding your skills. More and more people are picking up cameras today than ever before. From home moviemakers to aspiring producers of action-sports videos, the number of participants is growing every year. This means that by keeping yourself ahead of the game — and creating projects that are unique, and possibly that even fill a void that hasn't been filled before — you'll be able to hold an edge against the competition.

Figure 12-5 *Action sports online with GrindTV.com.*

The first key to finding that success is motivation. You have to consider what it is that you truly want to accomplish — and you have to mean it. Earlier in the book, we looked at the idea that many people have great ideas, but very few people execute those ideas. This holds true in every facet of life. Each day, thousands, if not millions, of original film ideas come up — and each day, only a handful of those people take action. You have to want it. Film may be one of the most competitive industries in the world, but thankfully, the niche of action-sports film-making is less so. There is room for new projects and original work in the industry. Do what you can to keep your eye on that ball, and then get to work making your film.

The second most critical step you'll encounter is scheduling your time. If you have a day job, are in school, or even focus your free time on an action sport, then you'll have to find a schedule that works for you and is realistic. When I took an entrepreneurial course in college, numerous company founders came in to lecture on how they found success. I remember one of them in particular: Paul Orfalea, who founded Kinko's in his garage while he was in college. In his lecture, Paul shared several basic concepts that have always stuck with me.

The first was that he put a major emphasis on time management. If you allot a fixed amount of time each day to developing your project, followed by a block of time on emails, then another block on other responsibilities, in the end, you'll get much more done. Too often people try to spend all of their day on a project, then, when general life responsibilities get in the way, they get frustrated or stressed.

The next key thing Paul said was that because he had dyslexia, he realized early on that he needed to hire people who were smarter than he was in his weak areas. This is a key in filmmaking as well. Don't try to do everything; instead, find someone who excels where you do not. If you know a great editor, then hire that person. If you are better at shooting than you are at producing, then find yourself a producer. If you surround yourself with good people in any project, it's only going to elevate the quality of the project.

Finally, Paul's story of getting started began in his garage in Santa Barbara. There was no enormous grant of money or big venture-capital fund to get him going. He took an original idea, filled a void that he saw, and did so simply and cheaply.

There is no better way to find success than to emulate those successful people who have come before us. Whether it's an action-sports documentary you are making or a new online series of webisodes, it all starts with your concept and your time and project management.

Setting Goals and Timelines

Having a clear goal requires a solid schedule. The best way to set one up is to consider, first, how long you anticipate the entire process to take. Second, set a deadline for the final project and be realistic about it. And finally, work backward from that deadline and break down monthly goals, weekly goals — and then, if necessary, even daily goals.

If you pick a deadline and just stare at it on your calendar, you're either going to wind up procrastinating and cramming to achieve it at the last minute, or, worse, front-load too much of the work and not give certain aspects of it the time and focus they deserve. Consider getting a calendar specific to that project. Put it in a place that you use for work and that you see regularly. Throughout the calendar, clearly label each goal deadline, beginning with small day-to-day tasks. If you're making an action-sports documentary, then set deadlines such as finding a producer by the end of the month. Then your small daily goals might be allotting two hours a day to researching producers, the project, and other key aspects of the process. When you approach that three-week mark, be sure you're getting close to achieving your first big deadline.

If, on the other hand, your intentions are simply to go out and shoot a video with your friends, then your goals can be as basic as shooting a minimum of six hours per week, or making sure you get to at least three different skate spots per week. It doesn't matter what the goal is, so long as it's realistic, you set it, and you stick to a schedule that'll get you there.

Jack-of-All-Trades, Master of None

We've all heard that expression, but what we rarely hear is the end of it. The original complete epithet reads: "Jack-of-all-trades, master of none, though oftentimes better than a master of one." Interestingly enough, the world is changing to a more complicated, more integrated place. This latter version of the saying, in its totality, puts the emphasis back on the benefit of being good at many things.

In the old days of filmmaking, a great cameraman could perhaps someday become a director of photography (DP), but never would he or she become an editor or a director. But that was then. Today, more and more filmmakers are climbing the ranks with a wealth of knowledge in all fields. From the aspiring director who is an excellent cameraman, editor, and even writer, to the action-sports filmmaker who literally does every aspect of the production alone, technology and knowledge of all fields have expanded so fast, and have become so affordable, that anyone can get involved and learn the arts.

There was a time in the past when large production companies and even studios were interested in hiring only that master of one trade. Today, countless companies are in search of young up-and-coming talent that can oversee the planning and execution of a shoot, as well as do creative work on how to incorporate web elements and other distribution opportunities.

We live in a world connected by virtual hotspots such as MySpace and YouTube; this is the stomping ground in which young filmmakers are cutting their teeth. This is also a distinctively different place from classic real-world spots: film festivals, production companies, and shooting locations. Both types of places, however, require a social and professional understanding of networking, etiquette, and skills. Twenty years ago, no one would have predicted that these two worlds would collide.

The future of action-sports filmmaking is a path that you cannot take, for it doesn't exist yet. No one could have imagined that Tony Hawk would land that 900 at the Summer X Games so long ago, and no one would have thought that action sports would be shot on high-def 24p cameras, but this is the world we live in. Where it goes from here is up to you.

Index